VANITY OF VANITIES

NOTES ON ECCLESIASTES

Andy Sochor

Gospel
Armory
PUBLISHING

Published by:
Gospel Armory Publishing
Bowling Green, Kentucky
www.GospelArmory.com

Printed in the United States of America

Cover photo by Matt DeVore, *Visions of Rapture Photography*
Used by permission

ISBN: 978-0-9831046-7-4

Preface

People want to live life with a purpose. Yet many, after trying to find fulfillment in various pursuits, eventually reach the conclusion that, in the end, their efforts, goals, and accomplishments are meaningless. They come to realize, as the wise man discovered, that *"all is vanity"* (Ecclesiastes 1:2).

Solomon did what many attempt to do – find purpose or fulfillment through the various pursuits of this life. His unique position allowed him to do whatever he chose to do and acquire whatever possessions he desired. But despite all of the riches and freedom he had, he could not find purpose in life. He was left with the inescapable conclusion: man's purpose is to *"fear God and keep His commandments"* (Ecclesiastes 12:13).

The book of Ecclesiastes contains lessons learned from the pursuit of wealth, wisdom, labor, and power. It shows us that real happiness and fulfillment are not obtained by focusing on life *under the sun*, but by looking past this life to what awaits our spirits after death.

My intent in writing this commentary was not to anticipate and address every question that might arise from the text. Such exhaustive commentaries, while valuable, can sometimes provide so much information that they become difficult to use and understand. My goal was to explain the text in a simple and concise way so that it can be easily used by all Bible students. I hope my efforts here will help you in your study of Ecclesiastes.

Table of Contents

Chapter 1

1:1   *The words of the Preacher, the son of David, king in Jerusalem.* Though not specifically named, the author of Ecclesiastes is clearly Solomon. The structure of this verse is similar to that in Proverbs 1:1 – *"The proverbs of Solomon the son of David, king of Israel."* Solomon is the Preacher of Ecclesiastes. In identifying himself as the Preacher, he makes it clear that these instructions are being taught to us and that they are intended for our learning. This is not a personal diary that was found which the author never intended for the contents in it to be shared with others in their original form. Solomon clearly indicates that he expects us to read his words and learn from them.

All is Vanity (1:2-11)

1:2   *"Vanity of vanities," says the Preacher, "Vanity of vanities! All is vanity."* The Preacher sets forth the topic to be discussed: the futility and insignificance of matters pertaining to this life. He repeats the phrase, *"vanity of vanities,"* for emphasis.

1:3   *What advantage does man have in all his work which he does under the sun?* Solomon uses a very different tone than he did in his writings in Proverbs: *"In all labor there is profit"* (Proverbs 14:23). Is the wise man contradicting himself? No, he is simply writing from a different perspective. He does not say here that there is no profit in labor. Rather, he asks what can be produced in our labor that has any true, lasting value. His perspective here is in regard to matters *"under the sun."* This is important. Nowhere does Solomon imply that our eternal existence is futile, only the secular pursuits of our earthly existence.

1:4   *A generation goes and a generation comes, but the earth remains forever.* Our lives here *under the sun* are temporary. The earth will remain as long as God sees fit to allow it to remain, but our years are insignificant in comparison.

1:5   *Also, the sun rises and the sun sets; and hastening to its place it rises there again.* Time, which is marked by the rising and setting of the sun, continues to move. It cannot be stopped or slowed down by man any more than one can stop or slow down the rotation of the earth.

1:6   *Blowing toward the south, then turning toward the north, the wind continues swirling along; and on its circular courses the wind returns.* One of the natural elements in weather is wind. Wind has direction. It has freedom. Yet it ultimately follows the same circuit.

1:7   *All the rivers flow into the sea, yet the sea is not full. To the place where the rivers flow, there they flow again.* The great volume of water that flows from the rivers into the oceans will never fill them up. This is an observation that harmonizes with the scientifically understood process of rainfall and evaporation: the water that runs through the rivers to the oceans will find itself back in the rivers again through the natural process which God has ordained. The water we have now is the same water which existed at the beginning. It continues to cycle through the system which God designed.

1:8   *All things are wearisome; man is not able to tell it. The eye is not satisfied with seeing, nor is the ear filled with hearing.* All that is done *under the sun* requires effort. Regardless of how much effort we exert or how weary we become, there will always be more to see and hear. The natural curiosity of mankind to see and hear new things will never be quenched.

1:9   *That which has been is that which will be, and that which has been done is that which will be done. So there is nothing new under the sun.* This is sort of a conclusion to the previous verses. There is a pattern to life. History repeats itself. Natural laws which God ordained in the beginning remain in place. Mankind generally follows the same habits from generation to generation.

1:10   *Is there anything of which one might say, "See this, it is new"? Already it has existed for ages which were before us.* Man is always looking for new and exciting things. While we may discover things that are new to our consciousness, our experience is very limited. We have no cause for arrogance on account of some "new" discovery we may have made.

1:11   *There is no remembrance of earlier things; and also of the later things which will occur, there will be for them no remembrance among those who will come later still.* Most people of the past have been forgotten, no matter what they did or how important they, or others, thought they were. The same will be true for us, our children, our children's children, and so on. If our goal in life is to be remembered after we depart, we have a futile goal.

Futility of Wisdom (1:12-18)

1:12   *I, the Preacher, have been king over Israel in Jerusalem.* Solomon was king over God's people during a time of great prosperity and peace. His peculiar circumstances allowed him to experiment and experience much of life, far more than any of us are able to do. If satisfaction and purpose could be found in this life, Solomon was in the best possible position to find it.

1:13   *And I set my mind to seek and explore by wisdom concerning all that has been done under heaven. It is a grievous task which God has given to the sons of men to be afflicted with.* Solomon was not merely curious about the purpose and meaning of life as most people are – he diligently sought out the answers. This laborious task has been given by God to the sons of men in two ways. First, He has instilled in man a curiosity to discover that which is unknown. Second, He has not revealed everything to man. Therefore, He has left us with unanswered questions, and by our curiosity, has given us the motivation to keep searching.

1:14   *I have seen all the works which have been done under the sun, and behold, all is vanity and striving after wind.* Again, Solomon's unique situation gave him the opportunity to experience much of life, so much so that he could say he had seen *"all the works that are done under the sun."* We are again reminded of the scope of this book: things that are done *"under the sun"* – not heavenly things, but earthly things; not spiritual things, but temporal. The pursuit of these things is vanity and striving after wind. Making an analogy to wind is helpful, as it easily illustrates the futility of the matters that pertain to this life. Wind cannot be restrained or controlled – that is out of our hands. Similarly, much of life is out of our control as well.

1:15 **What is crooked cannot be straightened and what is lacking cannot be counted.** This world is not perfect. There are things in life that are crooked. There are other things that are *wanting* or *lacking.* Solomon in all his investigations could see the inequity, injustice, suffering, and difficulties of life. But though he could recognize them, they could not be *straightened* or *numbered* (brought to completeness). Man is incapable of reforming this world into some sort of utopian paradise, despite having the best of intentions. It will always be lacking.

1:16 **I said to myself, "Behold, I have magnified and increased wisdom more than all who were over Jerusalem before me; and my mind has observed a wealth of wisdom and knowledge."** Solomon recognized the great wisdom he had in comparison with those who came before him. This is not an arrogant statement, for God had blessed him with this great wisdom (1 Kings 3:12). There was none who could rival him in regard to wisdom or knowledge.

1:17   *And I set my mind to know wisdom and to know madness and folly; I realized that this also is striving after wind.* Solomon was not just given wisdom, he desired wisdom and set his mind to acquire it. He also says he experienced *madness* and *folly*. No matter what direction he took, he discovered that there was no real fulfillment or satisfaction to be found in this life.

1:18   *Because in much wisdom there is much grief, and increasing knowledge results in increasing pain.* As one grows in wisdom, the truths that Solomon writes about become more clear, creating a stronger awareness of the futility of life. As one grows in knowledge, he becomes more aware of those things which cannot be discovered. Focusing on these things, without remembering God, will only result in grief and sorrow.

Chapter 2

Futility of Pleasures and Possessions (2:1-11)

2:1-2 *I said to myself, "Come now, I will test you with pleasure. So enjoy yourself." And behold, it too was futility. I said of laughter, "It is madness," and of pleasure, "What does it accomplish?"* After finding no lasting fulfillment in the sober pursuit of wisdom, Solomon moves to the light-hearted realm of pleasure and the care-free enjoyment of life. It seems that this is the natural progression for many men who search for purpose and satisfaction in life. When the thoughtful, diligent quest to increase in wisdom and knowledge leaves one lacking, many turn to these types of pursuits. Yet Solomon found that laughter, pleasure, and enjoyment were not only futile; but for one to be wholly given to these things was foolishness.

2:3 *I explored with my mind how to stimulate my body with wine while my mind was guiding me wisely, and how to take hold of folly, until I could see what good there is for the sons of men to do under heaven the few years of their lives.* Solomon then turned to alcohol. But despite the already depressing tone of this book, he did not turn to the destructive abuse of alcohol like so many do. Rather, he did what some do today (or attempt to do): he used alcohol (*wine*) to cheer himself and to get his mind off of his troubles. Yet he limited his use of alcohol such that he could still follow after wisdom. Not only do the Scriptures warn us against the casual use of alcohol (cf. Proverbs 23:31; 1 Peter 4:3), but Solomon testifies here of the fact that alcohol cannot solve any of our problems. It only provides a temporary distraction. It delays the necessary task of confronting our problems and dealing with difficult questions. If one seeks to discover *"what good there is for the sons of men to do,"* the answer will not be found in wine or any other similar drink. Finding the answers and purpose for life will only be delayed by such use of alcohol.

2:4-6 *I enlarged my works: I built houses for myself, I planted vineyards for myself; I made gardens and parks for myself and I planted in them all kinds of fruit trees; I made ponds of water for myself from which to irrigate a forest of growing trees.* Man often judges his own sense of worth based upon what he has made or what he possesses. Solomon had far more in this regard than most men who have ever lived. Yet such things could not bring lasting satisfaction. Part of Solomon's problem was that his pursuits were self-centered (*"for myself"*). As he explains later, there is nothing wrong with enjoying the blessings one has in life (5:18-19). But when one's entire focus is on *self*, he will never be complete.

2:7 *I bought male and female slaves and I had homeborn slaves. Also I possessed flocks and herds larger than all who preceded me in Jerusalem.* The number of one's servants and the size of one's flocks were other ways to judge the wealth and success of an individual. Just as he had with wisdom (1:16), Solomon had exceeded those who preceded him in Jerusalem.

2:8   *Also, I collected for myself silver and gold and the treasure of kings and provinces. I provided for myself male and female singers and the pleasures of men — many concubines.* Solomon accumulated riches. As the king he had authority to collect taxes and treasure from other kings and provinces. He had more wealth than we could dream of having here. Often we are tempted to say that we would be satisfied if we just had "more," yet Solomon was not satisfied with the greatest wealth one could hope to obtain. He took pleasure in music, but this was nothing more than a distraction. He had *"seven hundred wives, princesses, and three hundred concubines"* (1 Kings 11:3), yet these did not bring satisfaction.

2:9   *Then I became great and increased more than all who preceded me in Jerusalem. My wisdom also stood by me.* Solomon was great in the sense that he possessed more than all who came before him. Despite his great wealth, he did not forget or forfeit the wisdom he had gained.

2:10   *All that my eyes desired I did not refuse them. I did not withhold my heart from any pleasure, for my heart was pleased because of all my labor and this was my reward for all my labor.* Whatever Solomon saw that he wanted, he was able to take possession of it and did so. Whatever he desired in his heart, he obtained for himself. In accumulating these possessions, Solomon says his heart was *pleased*. There was a degree of satisfaction, even though it would not last. This is what fools people: the temporary satisfaction that comes from the pursuits of this life. Many will mistake this *temporary* satisfaction for *real* satisfaction. Yet at some point, the realization will come that these things are vain and futile. But while one focuses on the here and now, he can, for a time, rejoice in obtaining what he desires. The wise man then says that these things – the temporary pleasures and benefits that exist *under the sun* – are the rewards for his labor.

2:11   *Thus I considered all my activities which my hands had done and the labor which I had exerted, and behold all was vanity and striving after wind and there was no profit under the sun.* Despite the pleasure and joy that could be obtained from the material things of this life, this is where one always finds oneself: realizing that such pursuits are vain and striving after the wind. Earlier, Solomon mentioned the *"circular courses"* of the wind (1:6). Despite its movement and appearance of freedom, the wind would ultimately accomplish nothing. So it is with all of our efforts and labor in this life. Anything accomplished *under the sun*, in the end, will get us no further than where we started.

Wisdom and Folly (2:12-17)

2:12   *So I turned to consider wisdom, madness and folly; for what will the man do who will come after the king except what has already been done?* After failing to find satisfaction in the pursuit of pleasures and possessions, the wise man turns back to wisdom, madness, and folly. He discussed these things in the previous chapter and concluded: *"this also is striving after wind"* (1:17). The previous discussion focused on the futility of wisdom (1:16-18). Here, he considers the future of the wise man compared with that of the fool. The second phrase of this verse reminds us of what he observed earlier: *"That which has been is that which will be, and that which has been done is that which will be done. So there is nothing new under the sun"* (1:9). Whoever would replace him as king would not be able to do any more than what Solomon had done.

2:13   *And I saw that wisdom excels folly as light excels darkness.* There is a clear, unmistakable difference between light and darkness. Furthermore, light is more powerful as it is able to drive darkness away. This is what Solomon observed in regard to wisdom and folly – wisdom is far greater and far more powerful than folly. Taken by itself, this verse seems to fit the tone of the book of Proverbs more than Ecclesiastes – emphasizing the benefits of wisdom, rather than the hardships and futility of life. Yet as Solomon continues, he quickly gets back to the futility and vanity of even as noble a pursuit as wisdom.

2:14   *The wise man's eyes are in his head, but the fool walks in darkness. And yet I know that one fate befalls them both.* The wise man is able to discern his path and will therefore avoid trouble whenever possible. The fool is in darkness, unable to see where he is going or what dangers lie ahead. Clearly, wisdom is to be preferred over folly. Yet as he looked to the future – namely death – Solomon saw the common link between the two. Both the wise man and the fool will suffer the same fate. Again, it is important to remember the perspective from which this book is written. It pertains to things *under the sun*. In this regard, there is no difference between the wise and the fool, even though, as Solomon will acknowledge later, there is a difference in the *eternal* fate of the wise man and the fool. But both the wise man and the foolish man will go to the grave at the end of this life.

2:15   *Then I said to myself, "As is the fate of the fool, it will also befall me. Why then have I been extremely wise?" So I said to myself, "This too is vanity."* For what purpose did Solomon *"set* [his] *mind to seek and explore by wisdom"* (1:13)? He would one day be dead, just as the fool would be. So he concluded that his diligent pursuit of wisdom was vanity.

2:16   *For there is no lasting remembrance of the wise man as with the fool, inasmuch as in the coming days all will be forgotten. And how the wise man and the fool alike die!* Solomon was a unique case. He is remembered and his words have been preserved because they are part of the Scriptures. But for the vast majority of people, what the wise man says here is true: whether you are wise or a fool, you will be forgotten. This has nothing to do with anyone personally, since *"in the coming days all will be forgotten."* Both the wise man and the fool will die. What, then, is the purpose of acquiring wisdom if we will not be remembered for it?

2:17   *So I hated life, for the work which had been done under the sun was grievous to me; because everything is futility and striving after wind.* Wisdom was the defining characteristic of Solomon. Yet this wisdom was not going to save him from the fate which awaited the fool – death. Therefore, Solomon says he *"hated life."* That which he diligently pursued was futility. It is frustrating and depressing for one to come to the realization that what he has worked diligently to accomplish is meaningless. This is the condition Solomon found himself in here. That which he had done *under the sun* was, as he discovered, *"futility and striving after wind."* Even wisdom, which is a good thing to pursue, if one does not look beyond this life, will seem to be futile.

Futility of Labor (2:18-26)

2:18   *Thus I hated all the fruit of my labor for which I had labored under the sun, for I must leave it to the man who will come after me.* The beginning of this chapter considered the labors of Solomon, and the wise man concluded, *"all was vanity and striving after wind and there was no profit under the sun"* (2:11). Here, he goes a step further. More than seeing the fruit of his labor as *vanity*, Solomon says he *"hated all the fruit of* [his] *labor."* The reason is that he will have to leave all these things to someone else. The next verse explains why this is a problem.

2:19   *And who knows whether he will be a wise man or a fool? Yet he will have control over all the fruit of my labor for which I have labored by acting wisely under the sun. This too is vanity.* There was no guarantee for Solomon that those things he gained from a lifetime of working would be used wisely by those who would come after him. They may act wisely or foolishly. As he noted in the book of Proverbs, *"A good man leaves an inheritance to his children's children"* (Proverbs 13:22). Yet there is no way to ensure that the children of the good man will act wisely, allowing the grandchildren to enjoy the fruit of his labor. At death, he surrenders control of his estate. The provisions he made for future generations may be quickly squandered.

2:20   ***Therefore I completely despaired of all the fruit of my labor for which I had labored under the sun.*** Solomon had already discovered that life was temporary and that one could find no lasting satisfaction in life. His last hope of finding fulfillment with the material rewards of work was that those who would come after him would be able to enjoy what he was able to provide them, thus leaving a remembrance of him in future generations. Yet he realized that his best intentions could be in vain.

2:21   ***When there is a man who has labored with wisdom, knowledge and skill, then he gives his legacy to one who has not labored with them. This too is vanity and a great evil.*** Accomplishing the things Solomon did required a great deal of work. Anything we earn for our labors in this life requires the things he mentioned: *wisdom, knowledge, and skill.* Yet the laborer who works diligently and exercises wisdom in order to be able to gain, acquire, or accomplish what he does, when he dies, will leave all of these things to another – one who did not work for them and will, therefore, not appreciate them or use them as wisely as the one who worked for them.

2:22-23 ***For what does a man get in all his labor and in his striving with which he labors under the sun? Because*** *all his days his task is painful and grievous; even at night his mind does not rest. This too is vanity.* What, then, is accomplished by all of our labors? The fruit of our labors cannot bring lasting fulfillment. The wealth we acquire will be left for others to squander. The accomplishments we make will be forgotten. So the wise man says that what we are left with are pain and stress. While the labor is being done, there is pain. During breaks from work, such as at night, there is stress and worry associated with work. The wise man notes that this is vanity.

2:24-25 *There is nothing better for a man than to eat and drink and tell himself that his labor is good. This also I have seen that it is from the hand of God. For who can eat and who can have enjoyment without Him?* Knowing, then, the futility of our labors and the hardships that they cause, Solomon says that a man must simply eat and drink and tell himself that what he is doing is good. While work is important, despite Solomon's depressing analysis, it is also proper to enjoy the blessings of this life. These blessings ultimately come from God. Without Him there would be no good things to enjoy.

2:26 *For to a person who is good in His sight He has given wisdom and knowledge and joy, while to the sinner He has given the task of gathering and collecting so that he may give to one who is good in God's sight. This too is vanity and striving after wind.* The beginning of this verse is similar to some of the thoughts expressed in the book of Proverbs in which emphasis is placed upon *righteousness* causing one to be blessed (in this case, blessed with wisdom, knowledge, and joy).

Wickedness would cause one not only to be cursed, but his calamity that would come as a result would further enrich the righteous. The wise man writes in Proverbs, *"The wealth of the sinner is stored up for the righteous"* (Proverbs 13:22). Yet even then, Solomon concludes that this is vanity. Focusing on life *under the sun*, the same fate awaits both the righteous and the wicked, regardless of their different circumstances in life.

Chapter 3

A Time for Everything (3:1-11)

3:1   *There is an appointed time for everything. And there is a time for every event under heaven—* When Solomon began this book, he spoke of the cyclical patterns that exist in life (the generations of man, the rotation of the earth, the movements of the wind, and the flow of the rivers). These are established patterns from which man is not able to break free.

3:2   *A time to give birth and a time to die; a time to plant and a time to uproot what is planted.* Every person goes through the same cycle of life. Though circumstances will be different in each person's life, what we all have in common is that we were born into this world and will one day depart through death. The wise man then mentions the annual cycle of planting, harvesting (which is implied), and uprooting the once fruitful plants in order to prepare the ground for the planting of new plants. Without this providential cycle (see Genesis 8:22), man would have no crops to enjoy.

3:3   *A time to kill and a time to heal; a time to tear down and a time to build up.* The wise man says that there is a time to kill. This is not a contradiction of the sixth commandment – *"You shall not murder"* (Exodus 20:13). Even the Law states that there are certain circumstances in which killing is not condemned and is sometimes even encouraged – cases of capital punishment (Exodus 21:12), military engagement (Deuteronomy 7:2), or self-defense (Exodus 22:2). Yet there are other times when *healing* is necessary. There will be times when works need to be broken down and other times when new works need to be built or old works need to be strengthened.

3:4   *A time to weep and a time to laugh; a time to mourn and a time to dance.* Weeping and mourning are for times of sorrow and loss. Laughter and dancing would be completely inappropriate during such occasions. However, there are other occasions that are more light-hearted and joyful in which weeping and mourning would be out of place. We must respond appropriately to each situation in which we find ourselves.

3:5   *A time to throw stones and a time to gather stones; a time to embrace and a time to shun embracing.* In order to *throw stones*, one must first *gather* them. The wise man's point is that for every good and necessary thing which we must do, there are certain tasks that must be done in order to *prepare* for them. There is also a proper and improper time for embracing. During certain circumstances, showing affection is good and necessary. Other times, these same gestures would be inappropriate.

3:6   *A time to search and a time to give up as lost; a time to keep and a time to throw away.* When there is something of value that is lost, we ought to search it out and find it, just as the woman of whom Jesus spoke who searched for her lost coin (Luke 15:8-9). However, if the missing item is worthless – or would require more time, energy, and resources to locate it than it would take to replace it – then it would be better to give up on our search for it. Keeping and throwing away something would also be based upon its value. Some things are valuable because of their usefulness or because of the value which others have placed upon it. Other things that are useless and worthless to others (therefore, we cannot sell them or trade them for something useful) need to be thrown away.

3:7   *A time to tear apart and a time to sew together; a time to be silent and a time to speak.* It is becoming a lost art for women in our society to work with their hands and make clothing or other such items. But the principle here can still be seen: there are times when something that is incomplete can be completed, and other times when a project needs to be started over from the beginning. This principle can be applied to many areas of life, from work to relationships. The fact that there is *"a time to be silent and a time to speak"* is widely understood, though often not practiced. There are some times when we need to speak up in order to offer a word of encouragement, comfort one in sorrow, teach and defend the truth, and so on. There are also times when speaking would only cause trouble and would be counterproductive. At these times, silence is necessary.

3:8   *A time to love and a time to hate; a time for war and a time for peace.* We need to show love to all men. But we must also *hate* sin, error, and rebellion against God (cf. Psalm 119:104). There are also times for war and peace. As Solomon was the king over the nation of

Israel, he was in the position of leading and defending the people against their enemies. During Solomon's reign, the nation enjoyed a period of peace. Yet prior to his reign, during the days of both his father David and the first king Saul, the nation experienced war and turmoil. Every nation will have times of war and peace, just as Israel did.

3:9-10   *What profit is there to the worker from that in which he toils? I have seen the task which God has given the sons of men with which to occupy themselves.* After listing all of these things which are to be done in their own time, the wise man returns to the question about the profitability of our labors here. The previous verses continue the theme of finding no escape from the patterns of life that exist from generation to generation. Even though there may be a time of war, eventually peace will come. Sometime later, war will come again. The same is true for all of the things mentioned in the preceding verses. Despite the fact that certain variables exist in life, when one looks at the big picture, he can see that life is vanity. The tasks we perform are only there to *occupy ourselves* and are of no profit *under the sun.*

3:11   *He has made everything appropriate in its time. He has also set eternity in their heart, yet so that man will not find out the work which God has done from the beginning even to the end.* Although our lives here are temporary, our spirits are eternal. God has put in man the desire to look past this life and seek for something better. This is why Solomon sought for purpose in the things he discusses in this book. It is why people today search for meaning and purpose in their lives. Yet without the revelation of God, man will not figure out this purpose on his own. People come up with various theories and philosophies about what we ought to be doing in life; yet eternal satisfaction and fulfillment can only be found through God.

Nothing Better than to Rejoice and Do Good (3:12-22)

3:12-13 *I know that there is nothing better for them than to rejoice and to do good in one's lifetime; moreover, that every man who eats and drinks sees good in all his labor—it is the gift of God.* While discussing the seasons of life and the futility of our pursuits *under the sun*, Solomon reminds us again of the fact that our blessings come from God (cf. 2:24). Understanding both the futility of life and the fact that what we have comes from God, it is good for us to do two things: enjoy the blessings which God has given and do good with those things with which we have been blessed. If we cannot see *"good in all* [our] *labor"* – by enjoying God's blessings and helping others – then the futility of work *under the sun* will eventually result in depression and apathy, leading to a cessation of work. Nowhere does Solomon teach we should give up and do nothing. We must recognize the good *and* the limitations of the things of this life, while seeking for that which is eternal.

3:14 *I know that everything God does will remain forever; there is nothing to add to it and there is nothing to take from it, for God has so worked that men should fear Him.* The wise man has already noted that our works are only temporary. All that we accomplish will one day be lost. In contrast, the works of God remain forever. Furthermore, they are *complete*, so that there is nothing to add or take away from that which He has done. His works also teach us a lesson: we should *fear Him*. As the works of man are temporary and the works of God are eternal, we must fear God for our eternal fate rests in His hands.

3:15   *That which is has been already and that which will be has already been, for God seeks what has passed by.* Solomon repeats the point he made at the beginning in which he concluded, *"There is nothing new under the sun"* (1:9). But he adds to this point here – *"God seeks what has passed by."* The cyclical nature of life is not a mistake but is what God intended. The patterns that exist in the natural world are there as a result of God's providence manifested in the laws He established from the beginning. The patterns that man falls into from generation to generation are the result of man exercising his free choice (which has been given by God) within a world that is governed by God's natural laws.

3:16   *Furthermore, I have seen under the sun that in the place of justice there is wickedness and in the place of righteousness there is wickedness.* This is another reminder of the deficiencies that exist in this life. Because man is fallible, wickedness exists in the place of righteousness. Where we would hope to see justice, whether by one man toward another or by some human ruler or judge sitting in judgment over others, wickedness exists. Man becomes corrupt and biased and is often ignorant of the law or of certain facts that might pertain to the matter upon which justice is being sought. Even when the goal is righteousness and justice, despite the best of intentions, wickedness often arises.

3:17   *I said to myself, "God will judge both the righteous man and the wicked man," for a time for every matter and for every deed is there.* Unlike fallible human beings who are incapable of rendering perfect justice, God is the perfect judge. The wise man reminds us that while justice is not always realized among men, *"God will judge both the righteous man and the wicked man"* and will deal with us appropriately, depending on how we have responded to the various circumstances and challenges that exist in life *under the sun.*

3:18-19 *I said to myself concerning the sons of men, "God has surely tested them in order for them to see that they are but beasts." For the fate of the sons of men and the fate of beasts is the same. As one dies so dies the other; indeed, they all have the same breath and there is no advantage for man over beast, for all is vanity.* God tests man through the various challenges of life. The wise man recognizes that there is a purpose in this: that man would recognize that he is but a beast. Solomon is not saying that there is no difference between man and beast, nor is he denying the existence of the human soul. We remember that man has been made in the image of God and was granted authority to rule over the beasts and all the earth (Genesis 1:27-28). Men and animals are alike only with respect to physical animation. Solomon's point is meant to humble those who rule over God's creation. While man is in a unique and privileged position, he is still accountable to God.

Furthermore, despite the fact that man rules over the beasts of the earth, he will still die, just as the beast dies. As we see the fact that life is fragile, we cannot help but be impressed with the reality that despite our position, our accomplishments, or our wisdom, we will die one day just like a dumb beast.

3:20-21 *All go to the same place. All came from the dust and all return to the dust. Who knows that the breath of man ascends upward and the breath of the beast descends downward to the earth?* The *"same place"* that man and beast go is the dust of the earth. The difference, however, is what happens when the body goes to the dust of the earth. Man has an eternal spirit. Animals do not. Solomon will say later, *"Then the dust will return to the earth as it was, and the spirit will return to God, who gave it"* (12:7). Man's spirit will return to God because it, like God, is eternal. The spirit (*breath*) of beasts *"descends downward to the earth"* because it is temporal just as the body is temporal. Man and beast both have life. But only man possesses a spirit that will exist after this life is over. Man is self-aware, self-conscious, and aware of his place in time. Animals lack these traits. When one fails to see past this life, and focuses solely on life *under the sun*, then his life and death become no different from that of the beasts.

3:22 *I have seen that nothing is better than that man should be happy in his activities, for that is his lot. For who will bring him to see what will occur after him?* Life is temporary. We do not know what will come after us. No one can predict the future or declare to us with certainly what will transpire after our departure from this life. Therefore, besides preparing our spirits for eternity (which the wise man has alluded to a couple of times thus far in the book and which is the goal toward which he continues to direct us), he says in this verse that we should be happy with our activities. There are certainly times when we cannot change our circumstances; but to whatever extent we can control the work and activities in which we are involved, we should strive to do what brings us temporary satisfaction. Our labors cannot bring lasting satisfaction (2:10-11), and the fruits of our labor will someday be left to someone else (2:18). Yet the fruits of our labor are blessings from God (3:13), and we should find the good that does exist in the work that we do here.

Chapter 4

Oppression and Rivalries (4:1-6)

4:1   *Then I looked again at all the acts of oppression which were being done under the sun. And behold I saw the tears of the oppressed and that they had no one to comfort them; and on the side of their oppressors was power, but they had no one to comfort them.* After briefly considering eternity (3:11), God's judgment of man (3:17), and the fact that fact that our spirits will remain after our bodies are dead and buried (3:21), the wise man returns to those things which pertain to life *under the sun.* In this verse he considers *"acts of oppression."* No matter how many generations come and go, there will still be people who are oppressed and in a situation that is nearly or completely hopeless – at least in this life. When the oppressed remember their hope after this life, there is relief. Paul would later make this point to the brethren in Thessalonica who were suffering persecution (2 Thessalonians 1:7). But for those oppressed people who will not or cannot look past this life, there is no comfort. Furthermore, Solomon says there is no comfort for the *oppressors* either. Though they have power and can abuse and take advantage of others, there is no lasting value or meaning for them. Their satisfaction in life is limited to what they can unjustly take from others.

4:2   *So I congratulated the dead who are already dead more than the living who are still living.* For both the powerful and those who are hopelessly oppressed by them, life is vanity. Therefore, Solomon congratulates the dead (both the powerful who have no hope beyond what they can take from others and the oppressed who will not look past their trouble to things spiritual and eternal) because they have escaped this bitter existence.

4:3   *But better off than both of them is the one who has never existed, who has never seen the evil activity that is done under the sun.* Solomon then goes one step further. Those who are dead have an advantage of not having to experience the bitterness of oppression any more. But even better is the one who has never existed. The dead, though they have escaped the pains of life, have still experienced them. Those who are never conceived will never have to experience those things.

4:4   *I have seen that every labor and every skill which is done is the result of rivalry between a man and his neighbor. This too is vanity and striving after wind.* Although a man's work and the fruit of his labor are vanity (2:11), there is, as the wise man says elsewhere, *"profit"* in *"all labor"* (Proverbs 14:23). As man receives the just reward for his hard work, it results in a *rivalry* or *envy* (KJV) from his neighbor. His neighbor's desire for the fruit of the labors of the hardworking man can be manifested in two ways. First, it may provoke him to work hard, as well, to enjoy the same rewards as his neighbor. In free markets we can see the great results of competition as work, services, and products continue to improve by necessity. Second, it may cause one who is lazy and refuses to work hard himself to hate his neighbor and become embittered about his success. In either case, whether one man's work leads his neighbor to work harder or attack his accomplishments, it is vanity.

4:5   *The fool folds his hands and consumes his own flesh.* This verse serves as another reminder that when we study the book of Ecclesiastes, particularly the passages that describe the futility of labor, Solomon is *not* advocating that one should throw up his hands and give up. Here he says that *the fool* sits idle. Despite the vanity of labor, it is not foolish to work hard. Later Solomon will make the point that we *should* work hard (9:10).

4:6   *One hand full of rest is better than two fists full of labor and striving after wind.* Balance is necessary. Idleness is foolish; yet filling our lives with labor is *striving after wind.* Hard work is good and necessary, but it is not the ultimate purpose of our existence. We ought to take some time for rest. It is good to take a break from our labors and, among other things, reflect upon the truths about which Solomon writes.

The Value of Human Relationships (4:7-12)

4:7-8   *Then I looked again at vanity under the sun. There was a certain man without a dependent, having neither a son nor a brother, yet there was no end to all his labor. Indeed, his eyes were not satisfied with riches and he never asked, "And for whom am I laboring and depriving myself of pleasure?" This too is vanity and it is a grievous task.* It is natural for parents to strive to leave an inheritance to their children (2 Corinthians 12:14) or grandparents for their grandchildren (Proverbs 13:22). This motivates them to work hard and be good stewards of their blessings so that they can pass them on to the next generation (or to some other family, such as a brother, if they do not have children). But for the one who has no one to whom he can leave his estate, what purpose is there for him to work long, hard hours? Solomon reminds us that while hard work is good and necessary, it is important to consider *why* we are working and whether our time (or at least some of it) would be better spent with a different focus.

4:9   *Two are better than one because they have a good return for their labor.* In the next few verses, the wise man lists four reasons why partnership and companionship with others is beneficial to us. This verse contains the first reason that *two are better than one:* there is a better return for their labor. Although Solomon has already discussed the futility of labor (2:18-23), he also has said we must do good and recognize that the fruits of our labor are blessings from God (3:12-13). Work is necessary in life *under the sun* so we can provide for ourselves and our families and be able to do good and share with others. As we try to do the best work we can do, the reality is that we are limited when we work alone. But when we work with another, simple tasks can be done much more quickly; and complex tasks can be done more easily as each person can contribute his own unique skills, experiences, and expertise.

4:10   *For if either of them falls, the one will lift up his companion. But woe to the one who falls when there is not another to lift him up.* The second reason that *two are better than one* is that when one falls into trouble, his companion is able to come to his aid. When things are going smoothly in life, it can be tempting at times to think that we can "go it alone." Yet problems will inevitably come. When they do, it is important to have others who can help. We should note that this companion who comes to his friend's aid is more than just an acquaintance; he is one who can be counted on to help when the need arises. We know many people as acquaintances who would not be there to help us in time of trouble. It is important to have some close friends who will be aware of our trouble and be willing to help. These verses are often used to discuss marriage, and rightly so. Though not about marriage exclusively, marriage is a good application of the truths contained in a couple of these verses (4:10-11). Husbands and wives are to help one another and enjoy a mutual benefit of such a partnership throughout life.

4:11   *Furthermore, if two lie down together they keep warm, but how can one be warm alone?* The third reason why *two are better than one* is that they can help one another during times when they are both suffering hardship. If both are cold, they will stay cold unless they come together to keep each other warm.

4:12   *And if one can overpower him who is alone, two can resist him. A cord of three strands is not quickly torn apart.* The fourth reason why *two are better than one* is that there is strength in numbers. When one is alone, he is vulnerable to attacks from an evildoer. When he is with his companion, the two of them are better able to resist the attacker. Furthermore, if there are three companions together, they enjoy an even greater security. Some have taken this verse, applied it to marriage, and supposed that the third strand in the cord is God. In other words, a husband and wife are able to help one another; but their marriage will be even stronger if they are both faithfully following the Lord. This is certainly true. However, I do not believe that Solomon is discussing marriage and God in this verse. Though we can see a more direct application to marriage in the previous two verses, this verse is speaking in more general terms about the benefits of human companions. One person is vulnerable. Two are able to resist an attack. Three are even stronger than two.

The Value of Wisdom (4:13-16)

4:13   *A poor yet wise lad is better than an old and foolish king who no longer knows how to receive instruction.* People value riches and power. Yet here the wise man makes a contrast between a king (who has riches and power) and a lad (who does not possess these things). Solomon says the lad is better. Why? He possesses wisdom. This verse reminds us that wisdom is more important and more valuable than riches and power. Furthermore, we can see that even a king is just a fallible human being as he will sometimes need *instruction*. Occasionally it becomes necessary for one in power to repent and change his positions. The *foolish king* will not receive instruction, implying that one who will receive instruction and change his mind when necessary is wise.

4:14　*For he has come out of prison to become king, even though he was born poor in his kingdom.* This verse and the two that follow serve as a reminder of the temporary nature of civil authority. One who has power will not have that power forever. Some have speculated that Solomon is referring to a specific person here. Joseph is a possibility, as he was put in prison, released, and placed in a position of authority in Egypt (Genesis 41). Some have supposed that the king in this verse is Abraham having escaped the *"old and foolish king"* (Nimrod) mentioned in the previous verse. This theory is based upon oral traditions and Rabbinical commentary of Old Testament passages. Regardless of the person to whom Solomon is referring, or if he even is referring to a specific person at all, the point is that power is uncertain. One who rules over the people may be replaced by an unlikely successor, even one who has previously been in prison or one who was born poor in the country.

4:15　*I have seen all the living under the sun throng to the side of the second lad who replaces him.* When one is in power, especially when he is a *"foolish king,"* the people are eager for anyone to replace him. So when one comes along who can replace the current king, even if it is one who was previously in prison or poverty, they flock to the new king.

4:16　*There is no end to all the people, to all who were before them, and even the ones who will come later will not be happy with him, for this too is vanity and striving*

after wind. This cycle will continue. Leaders once eagerly supported by the people will eventually become unpopular. This might be due to the fickle nature of public opinion (which certainly exists) or because those who obtain power often become corrupt. The *"wise lad"* who replaces *"an old and foolish king"* may become an old and foolish king himself one day. So Solomon concludes that such rule and civil authority is *vanity* and *striving after wind*.

Chapter 5

Service to God (5:1-7)

5:1   *Guard your steps as you go to the house of God and draw near to listen rather than to offer the sacrifice of fools; for they do not know they are doing evil.* When the wise man speaks of going to the house of God, he is referring to worship. His warning is that we must be careful when we worship the Lord, for not every kind of worship we offer will be accepted by Him. The way we can know what will be pleasing to Him is by *drawing near to listen.* We must examine the word of God to know what He expects us to do. Many, however, do not want to consult the Scriptures or find out whether or not their plans will please the Lord. They offer worship and do those things that they think will be accepted. Yet in their presumptuousness, they violate the law of God, thus making it so that they *"offer the sacrifice of fools."* This is especially dangerous because they *"do not know they are doing evil."* Without seeing their error, they will only persist in it. Therefore, we must be very careful how we worship. God will not accept just anything we place within the context of worship.

5:2   *Do not be hasty in word or impulsive in thought to bring up a matter in the presence of God. For God is in heaven and you are on the earth; therefore let your words be few.* In addition to our actions in worship, Solomon says we must be careful that our words do not cause us to be condemned. As God is in heaven and we are on earth, we should understand that He is in a much greater position than we are and is worthy of the highest honor. This would be sound advice for our behavior before a human ruler, yet God is infinitely more worthy of honor and reverence. As we would guard our speech when in the presence of a human ruler, much more should we guard our speech before the Lord.

5:3   *For the dream comes through much effort and the voice of a fool through many words.* The effort (*business*, KJV) in which we are engaged in this life, as we focus on it and work at it, inevitably works its way into our dreams. The dreams are an indication of the amount of focus that has been placed upon our various endeavors. In the same way, the *"many words"* that are spoken are an indication that the voice speaking them is that of a fool. Discretion and self-control must be exercised if one wishes to show himself to be wise and not a fool.

5:4-5   *When you make a vow to God, do not be late in paying it; for He takes no delight in fools. Pay what you vow! It is better that you should not vow than that you should vow and not pay.* To understand this verse, it is important to remember the law regarding vows: *"You shall be careful to perform what goes out from your lips, just as you have voluntarily vowed to the Lord your God, what you have promised"* (Deuteronomy 23:23). The vows to which Solomon is referring are these vows that are made *voluntarily.* Because they are not commanded, it would be better to not vow than to make a vow and not be able to fulfill it. In the first case, no sin is committed because making the vow is voluntary. However, one who vows and fails to keep it has violated his promise, thus making him guilty. So Solomon says that before one makes a vow, he must be sure he can fulfill the vow. If he cannot fulfill it, he should not make it.

5:6   *Do not let your speech cause you to sin and do not say in the presence of the messenger of God that it was a mistake. Why should God be angry on account of your voice and destroy the work of your hands?* Again, Solomon says that carefulness must be exercised in regard to one's speech. When one vows, he must fulfill it. If he cannot fulfill it, making excuses such as, *"it was a mistake,"* will not justify him. Although no sin would be committed in *not* vowing, when one vows, God will hold him accountable.

5:7   *For in many dreams and in many words there is emptiness. Rather, fear God.* Solomon again mentions the *dreams* and *many words* that he has discussed earlier (5:3). Both of these are vanity. The dreams are nothing but thoughts and imaginations. Even when they reflect real life, they are not real themselves (and besides, the realities that they reflect are vanity, as he has already discussed at length). The many words (of a fool, as the context implies) are also vanity in that they do not amount to anything significant. Instead, we must fear God. This is the second time Solomon mentions this portion of the conclusion that he will eventually draw (cf. 3:14; 12:13).

Civil Authorities (5:8-9)

5:8   *If you see oppression of the poor and denial of justice and righteousness in the province, do not be shocked at the sight; for one official watches over another official, and there are higher officials over them.* Solomon has earlier spoken of the inevitability of oppression (4:1) and wickedness in the place of justice and righteousness (3:16). We should not be shocked when these conditions exist. The wise man gives one reason here: government bureaucracy. An extensive network/ hierarchy of officials who oversee the people is incapable of doing what they are supposed to do. The larger the bureaucracy, the more unaccountable and inefficient it becomes. It is important to note that this is not the observation of one who was a "common man" and was a victim of an ineffective government bureaucracy. It is the observation of Solomon, the head of the government. In his position, he could see that such an arrangement would not work to help the people. When there is a large bureaucracy in place, the wise man says we should expect the poor to be oppressed and justice and righteousness to be denied.

5:9   *After all, a king who cultivates the field is an advantage to the land.* The New American Standard translation can seem a little confusing on this verse. In the King James Version it reads: *"Moreover the profit of the earth is for all: the king himself is served by the field."* God created this world so that it would produce the food necessary to sustain life (Genesis 1:11-12, 29; Acts 14:17). A king, despite his position of authority over others, does not have the right to the fruit of the land over those who are in the fields working for it. This contains a reminder for those in authority: despite their position, they are just like the rest of us, relying upon God's providence to survive. So a wise king, rather than oppressing his people and burdening them with the support of an excessive bureaucracy (5:8), will allow the land to be cultivated and allow the people to enjoy the fruits of their labor, knowing that this is a benefit to him as well. The New American Standard translation does emphasize another point: *"A king who cultivates the field is an advantage to the land."* If the king, like everyone else, is a producer rather than requiring such a heavy burden from the people, he benefits the land in that way. Whichever translation one uses, an underlying point is the same: the king, despite his authority, is no different from his fellow man. If a ruler understands this, it benefits all. If he does not, it results in difficulties for the citizens of the land.

Futility of Riches (5:10-20)

5:10   *He who loves money will not be satisfied with money, nor he who loves abundance with its income. This too is vanity.* Solomon has earlier discussed his realization that the fruits of his labor are vanity (2:18-23). Here he returns to warning about the limitations of the fruits of man's labor, specifically in regard to money (silver, KJV). One who loves money, even if he obtains it, will never be satisfied. There will always be others with wealth greater than our own. There will always be things which we desire but lack the necessary funds to purchase. Furthermore, as Solomon will discuss in the following verses, money has a limited benefit. It does not solve every problem.

5:11 *When good things increase, those who consume them increase. So what is the advantage to their owners except to look on?* The phrase, *"those who consume,"* is parallel to the working man in the next verse. When a rich man is prosperous, he must employ more workers or servants to labor in his fields, tend to his possessions, oversee his operations, etc. These people rightfully deserve to be paid for their work, and the rich man must take them into account. So even though he becomes more prosperous, he must support more people. Therefore, all he can do is look on and see the work being done.

5:12 *The sleep of the working man is pleasant, whether he eats little or much; but the full stomach of the rich man does not allow him to sleep.* As we compare these two men, the working man has a relatively simple life. He puts in an honest day's work, earns a living, and is able to support his family. When he pillows his head at night, his sleep can be *pleasant* because he can take comfort in the fact that he is taking care of those things that he needs to do in this life. On the other hand, *the full stomach of the rich man does not allow him to sleep.* He has more to take care of, more to support (such as his workers), more to worry about, and more to lose. The stress that comes from his riches keeps him awake at night.

5:13-14 *There is a grievous evil which I have seen under the sun: riches being hoarded by their owner to his hurt. When those riches were lost through a bad investment and he had fathered a son, then there was nothing to support him.* Solomon is not saying that it is foolish or wrong for one to save his money. His point is that riches are uncertain. If one is careful with his money and saves it, all of his riches could still be lost through one bad investment. Then, despite his work in earning his wealth and his diligence in saving it, he will have nothing to leave to his children.

5:15-16 *As he had come naked from his mother's womb, so will he return as he came. He will take nothing from the fruit of his labor that he can carry in his hand. This also is a grievous evil—exactly as a man is born, thus will he die. So what is the advantage to him who toils for the wind?* The riches of this life are temporary. Just as man possesses nothing when he is born, he will take nothing with him when he leaves this world. Whatever he has gained here will remain. Therefore, the *advantage* that comes from one toiling for the wind is limited and temporary; and we must understand that fact. Solomon calls this a *grievous evil*. Of course, the fact that we brought nothing into this world and can take nothing out of it is what God intended (cf. 1 Timothy 6:7). The wise man is not saying that God's plan is evil. Rather, he is speaking of the perspective of the worldly man – *"He who loves money"* (5:10). To this man, the fact that his riches are temporary is evil because he has devoted all his time and energy in this life to obtain them and has no other hope.

5:17 *Throughout his life he also eats in darkness with great vexation, sickness and anger.* The darkness refers to a lack of enlightenment. The one who loves money does not realize the temporary and uncertain nature of riches, nor that the true purpose of man has to do with matters that are far more important than money. Because he is *in darkness* about this, his life is filled with *vexation, sickness, and anger*.

5:18   *Here is what I have seen to be good and fitting: to eat, to drink and enjoy oneself in all one's labor in which he toils under the sun during the few years of his life which God has given him; for this is his reward.* Understanding the vanity of riches and the futility of worrying about them, Solomon does not say that one ought to give up and do no work at all. Rather he says that it is good for one to simply enjoy the fruits of his labor in this life. These blessings are from God; and it is perfectly acceptable to enjoy these blessings, provided that we remember that they are temporary and that our purpose involves something that is higher and eternal.

5:19   *Furthermore, as for every man to whom God has given riches and wealth, He has also empowered him to eat from them and to receive his reward and rejoice in his labor; this is the gift of God.* This verse ought to remind us that riches are not evil. Solomon has been discussing one who *"loves money"* (5:10), not simply one who *has* money. The apostle Paul makes a similar point when he writes, *"For the love of money is a root of all sorts of evil"* (1 Timothy 6:10). Notice that money itself is not evil, but *"the love of money"* is. Those who have *riches and wealth* have been blessed by God. It is right and good for them to enjoy these blessings.

5:20   *For he will not often consider the years of his life, because God keeps him occupied with the gladness of his heart.* The one who recognizes that his riches are a blessing from God and enjoys them as such will not lament that the years of his life are short. He will enjoy God's blessings here and place his trust in God beyond this life. The one who *"loves money"* (5:10) does not enjoy his wealth because he is too consumed with worry over it and trying to accumulate more. Therefore, he does not consider or prepare for anything beyond this life.

Chapter 6

Futility of Life (6:1-12)

6:1-2 *There is an evil which I have seen under the sun and it is prevalent among men—a man to whom God has given riches and wealth and honor so that his soul lacks nothing of all that he desires; yet God has not empowered him to eat from them, for a foreigner enjoys them. This is vanity and a severe affliction.* What Solomon writes about here is *prevalent*: a man with riches, wealth, and honor, so that his soul lacks nothing, cannot enjoy or take advantage of his blessings. The reason why this man does not enjoy these blessings is not because he *chooses* to give them away or save them so that he can leave them for his children. Instead, a foreigner enjoys them. This is *evil*. The wise man is not suggesting that God does evil or has evil motives, but that this *condition* is evil. God's design is that the recipients of His blessings get to enjoy those blessings (3:13; 5:19), though He does allow one to suffer consequences from his own foolishness and from injustice at the hands of others who would take this man's blessings. It is good, of course, for one not only to enjoy his own blessings but to use his blessings for good (3:12; 5:13). But for one to have his blessings taken from him by force, even under the guise of aiding a foreigner, is evil.

6:3-5   *If a man fathers a hundred children and lives many
years, however many they be, but his soul is not
satisfied with good things and he does not even have a
proper burial, then I say, "Better the miscarriage than
he, for it comes in futility and goes into obscurity; and
its name is covered in obscurity. It never sees the sun
and it never knows anything; it is better off than he.*
When Solomon speaks of the oppression that exists in
life, he mentions two groups who are better off than
the living: the dead (4:2) and those who have not yet
existed (4:3). Similarly, he compares a certain man to a
child who was miscarried. He uses the miscarriage to
emphasize *futility* and *obscurity*. The man who *"fathers a
hundred and children and lives many years"* is surely
blessed. The Bible speaks of children and long life as
being blessings from God (Psalm 127:3-5; 91:16). But
despite being greatly blessed, if the man is not satisfied
with good things, he lives in *futility*. If he does not have
a proper burial, despite fathering a hundred children, it
would be because his children are not around (whether
due to death, abandonment, or having never learned a
proper respect for their father) to see to it that he
receives a proper burial. Therefore, he departs in
obscurity. If futility and obscurity are to mark one's life
and any remembrance of it, Solomon says, *"better the
miscarriage than he."*

6:6   *Even if the other man lives a thousand years twice and
does not enjoy good things—do not all go to one
place?"* The wise man has just spoken of one who is
not satisfied with good things as having a futile
existence. Here he considers it from a different angle.
No matter how long one lives on the earth, how richly
or poorly he is blessed here, whether or not he enjoys

and is satisfied with the good things of his life, *"all go to one place"* – the grave.

6:7   ***All a man's labor is for his mouth and yet the appetite is not satisfied.*** Solomon describes a principle that has existed from the beginning: man works in order to provide for himself. Yet his *appetite* is not satisfied. After he has eaten, he will later be hungry again. The work to provide for one's needs is an ongoing process.

6:8   ***For what advantage does the wise man have over the fool? What advantage does the poor man have, knowing how to walk before the living?*** There is certainly an advantage to having wisdom. Solomon concluded earlier that *"wisdom excels folly as light excels darkness"* (2:13). Yet, he knew that *"one fate befalls them both"* (2:14). It does not matter whether one is wise or foolish, rich or poor, all will depart from this life the same as everyone else.

6:9   ***What the eyes see is better than what the soul desires. This too is futility and a striving after wind.*** When people find no lasting purpose or meaning in the things they have seen or obtained in this life, many of them conclude that the thing they are missing that will bring their life meaning is something *under the sun*. So they long for more and more things that they do not have. But the wise man says that what one has is better than what one *desires to have* (focusing solely on this life, of course).

6:10   ***Whatever exists has already been named, and it is known what man is; for he cannot dispute with him who is stronger than he is.*** Solomon began this book by describing how there is *"nothing new under the sun"* (1:9). Each man is simply one of a generation that rises in place of the one before it, only to be replaced later by a new generation. Man *"comes in futility and goes in obscurity"* (6:4). The one who is stronger than *he* (man in general) is God. Man cannot *dispute* or *contend* (KJV) with God over the shortcomings, hardships, and futility that exist in this life. It is as Paul writes: *"On the contrary, who are you, O man, who answers back to God? The thing molded will not say to the molder, 'Why did you make me like this,' will it?"* (Romans 9:20). God created man and life on earth for a purpose. One who wishes to *contend* with God over it has not yet learned or does not yet fully appreciate the purpose that God has given man in this life.

6:11   *For there are many words which increase futility. What then is the advantage to a man?* The wise man has been discussing many *things* (KJV) which increase futility. We may try to increase and excel in such things as wisdom, wealth, labor, and pleasures. But in the end, our fate (death) is the same.

6:12   *For who knows what is good for a man during his lifetime, during the few years of his futile life? He will spend them like a shadow. For who can tell a man what will be after him under the sun?* Life is uncertain. We do not know, from day to day, what will be in store for us. Our life is *like a shadow*, or, as James describes it, it is like *"a vapor that appears for a little while and then vanishes away"* (James 4:14). Not only is life uncertain, but it is also short and filled with futile endeavors. So Solomon asks the question: *What is good for a man during his lifetime?* He is slowly but surely directing his readers toward the conclusion that he eventually reaches. This is important because up to this point, knowing the futility and vanity of life, there is no pursuit of life that is of any real value. We must look past the *few years* of our *futile lives* which we spend *like a shadow*. As Solomon will eventually explain plainly, we must look past this life to things that are eternal and provide real satisfaction and fulfillment.

Chapter 7

Various Proverbs (7:1-14)

7:1   *A good name is better than a good ointment, and the*
       day of one's death is better than the day of one's birth.
       A good name refers to one's character and reputation.
       Solomon compares it with *ointment*. This same word is
       used later to refer to *"a perfumer's oil"* (10:1). This is
       designed to provide a pleasing odor in order to mask
       an unpleasant one. A man of good character and
       reputation will not have unpleasant characteristics or
       sins that need to be masked, thus making the
       "ointment" unnecessary. This *ointment* or *oil* might also
       used for *anointing* as a sign of honor. Though one may
       be honored by such, it pales in comparison with the
       honor that comes from a blameless life. The wise man
       also says that the day of one's death is better than the
       day of one's birth. Looking at it solely from an earthly
       perspective, understanding the futility of life that the
       wise man has been discussing, death is preferable
       because it marks the end of one's struggles *under the*
       sun. But as we look beyond this life, which is where
       Solomon is directing us, this statement holds true as
       well *if* one has been upright and blameless, just as he
       must be to have the *good name* in the first place.

7:2   *It is better to go to a house of mourning than to go to a*
       house of feasting, because that is the end of every man,

and the living takes it to heart. Solomon is not saying here that it is wrong to feast, celebrate, and enjoy the things of this life. Such things have their time (3:4). But he says it is *better* to go to the house of mourning – the time and place where the dead are remembered. This is preferable because all go to this same place (6:6). Funerals and other similar occasions remind us of the brevity of life. We need to remember this. But why, if our existence is nothing but *vanity* and *futility*? This verse again provides a subtle reminder that while our life *under the sun* is futile, our existence as a whole is not. We need to remember that there is more to look forward to than our life here on the earth.

7:3　*Sorrow is better than laughter, for when a face is sad a heart may be happy.* This verse must be understood in light of the previous one. When one is in sorrow, he is better able to seriously consider important matters. Laughter provides a distraction from more serious matters. This is why Solomon wrote earlier, *"I said of laughter, 'It is madness'"* (2:2). One who is given to laughter, who never has a sad face, will not soberly consider his eternal fate. But when one's *"face is sad"* and he is in *sorrow*, he is in the proper state of mind to consider his true purpose in life. Though he may outwardly appear sorrowful, his *"heart may be happy."* This means he might have the satisfaction of knowing *why* he is here and *where* he is going.

7:4　*The mind of the wise is in the house of mourning, while the mind of fools is in the house of pleasure.* This verse reinforces verse two. One who is wise appreciates the benefits of the house of mourning. One who is foolish does not see the benefits and only wishes to occupy the house of pleasure.

7:5   *It is better to listen to the rebuke of a wise man than for one to listen to the song of fools.* Solomon continues building his case that man must prepare for something important after this life. Paul would later write, *"If the dead are not raised, let us eat and drink, for tomorrow we die"* (1 Corinthians 15:32). If life *under the sun* is futile (which Solomon has been explaining how it is) and we recognize this, what is there to live for? Many of those who refuse to look past this life will simply get as much enjoyment as they can out of life. These are the ones who *"listen to the song of fools."* On the other hand, if we recognize that life here is futile and there is something better that awaits us, then we need to be sure we live in such a way that will bring us the reward. Therefore, we *"listen to the rebuke of a wise man,"* understanding the value of eliminating sin from our lives and following after the wisdom that comes from above.

7:6   *For as the crackling of thorn bushes under a pot, so is the laughter of the fool; and this too is futility.* Thorn bushes do not make a good source of fuel for one who wishes to cook his food. Yet these thorn bushes will make a lot of noise while they are burning. The laughter of the fool is the same way. It does not amount to anything useful and is simply noise.

7:7   *For oppression makes a wise man mad, and a bribe corrupts the heart.* Solomon has spoken about oppression earlier, noting that those who are dead and those who have never existed are in a preferable position for not presently enduring such oppression (4:1-3). Even a wise man can be driven to madness by the oppression that exists among men. Furthermore, a bribe (*gift*, KJV) can corrupt the heart of an otherwise righteous man, thus convincing him to act in a wicked, often oppressive, manner.

7:8   *The end of a matter is better than its beginning; patience of spirit is better than haughtiness of spirit.* The satisfaction of a job that has come to completion is better than the prospect of completing the task before it has begun. But it is important to consider this in light of what was said at the beginning of the chapter. The end of a matter – one's death – is better than its beginning – one's birth (7:1). Solomon then says that *patience* is better than *haughtiness*, or arrogance. The arrogant man will reject any *"rebuke of a wise man"* (7:5) and will do only what seems best to him at the time. The one who is patient will look past what is immediately before him, consider his life and his fate, be willing to accept rebuke, and make correction.

7:9   *Do not be eager in your heart to be angry, for anger resides in the bosom of fools.* It seems as though some people look for reasons to be upset with others. The wise man tells us that we must not look for opportunities to be angry or to quickly react harshly when a wrong (or perceived wrong) is committed against us. Anger is a trait of the foolish man, not the wise man. The wise man learns how to control his emotions better than that.

7:10   *Do not say, "Why is it that the former days were better than these?" For it is not from wisdom that you ask about this.* It is not uncommon to hear people speak fondly of the "good old days." While reminiscing of days gone by may be fine, Solomon tells us that it is foolish to make unfair comparisons between the present and the past. He said earlier, *"That which has been is that which will be, and that which has been done is that which will be done. So there is nothing new under the sun"* (1:9). The reality is that every stage in life will have good times and bad times. The wise man warns against one deceiving himself into thinking that the *"former days"* were wholly good and that the present is full of trouble. Circumstances certainly change, but there will be both good and bad in every time if we will only look for it.

7:11-12 *Wisdom along with an inheritance is good and an advantage to those who see the sun. For wisdom is protection just as money is protection, but the advantage of knowledge is that wisdom preserves the lives of its possessors.* If one is able to gain both wisdom and money (*an inheritance*), he will certainly be in a good position. Both will provide a certain amount of protection for him. But wisdom is to be preferred since it is able to help us in ways that money cannot.

7:13 *Consider the work of God, for who is able to straighten what He has bent?* God has made us for a purpose. He has created this world, has blessed us, and also has allowed us to suffer hardship and oppression for a reason. We cannot change what God has done. We must simply accept His sovereignty, follow Him, and learn how to handle the challenges that exist in our life *under the sun.*

7:14   *In the day of prosperity be happy, but in the day of adversity consider—God has made the one as well as the other so that man will not discover anything that will be after him.* It is natural for one to rejoice during periods of prosperity. The wise man says here that we ought to rejoice in this. After all, such prosperity is *"the gift of God"* (5:19). Yet there will also be times of adversity. When these times come, we are not to become angry with God and rebel against Him, nor should we become depressed and think of our cause as now being hopeless. Instead, we must *consider* that fact that God is in control and there are lessons to be learned and responsibilities to be carried out in each phase of life. This uncertainty of life exists in order to remind us that we cannot know what the future holds. Therefore, we must look to God, place our trust in Him, and serve Him regardless of our current circumstances.

Observations on a Life of Futility (7:15-29)

7:15   *I have seen everything during my lifetime of futility; there is a righteous man who perishes in his righteousness and there is a wicked man who prolongs his life in his wickedness.* Solomon again reminds us of his great experience in all that he has seen in his life. He noticed that good people (the righteous) died in their righteousness – he implies that they died young and/or in the midst of unfortunate circumstances. Conversely, he saw that the wicked enjoyed life for many years. Coupling this verse with the one before it, we can learn the truth that good and bad things happen to all people. Therefore, we should not think of one's circumstances as necessarily being an accurate gauge for his righteousness before God. Neither physical prosperity nor misfortune can be necessarily ascribed to God.

7:16   *Do not be excessively righteous and do not be overly wise. Why should you ruin yourself?* This verse may seem difficult at first glance. Why does Solomon tell us not to be *"excessively righteous"* or *"overly wise"*? Is it possible to be *too* righteous or *too* wise? No. His point, as E. M. Zerr explains in his commentary, is about being an extremist. An extremist is not one who simply follows the will of God faithfully in all things. Rather, an extremist goes beyond God's standard and establishes his own standard of righteousness – much like the Pharisees we read about in the New Testament. The wise man is warning us against trusting in ourselves and our own wisdom rather than relying upon God. These same warnings are given in the writings of Proverbs (cf. Proverbs 3:5-7).

7:17   *Do not be excessively wicked and do not be a fool. Why should you die before your time?* Solomon is not saying that a little bit of wickedness is acceptable. Instead, he is continuing his point about extremism. One may be wicked, yet not destroy his physical life (7:15). Yet one who is *"excessively wicked"* will jeopardize his physical life (hence the mention of premature death), as well as jeopardizing his soul.

7:18   *It is good that you grasp one thing and also not let go of the other; for the one who fears God comes forth with both of them.* This is Solomon's conclusion to the previous verses: one should not go to either extreme –

becoming so "righteous" that he seeks to establish his own righteousness or becoming so wicked that his life is in danger.

7:19   *Wisdom strengthens a wise man more than ten rulers who are in a city.* This verse is another reminder of the value of wisdom, proving again that the warning against being *"overly wise"* (7:16) is about the wisdom of man. This verse is addressing divine wisdom that comes from following God's ways. This wisdom is more beneficial to us than ten rulers in a city. Following God is of much greater benefit to us than any help we can derive from human governments.

7:20   *Indeed, there is not a righteous man on earth who continually does good and who never sins.* This verse is a lot like what Paul writes in Romans 3:23 – *"For all have sinned and fall short of the glory of God."* Solomon is not excusing or justifying sin, but is simply stating the reality that all men must continue to battle against sin.

7:21-22 *Also, do not take seriously all words which are spoken, so that you will not hear your servant cursing you. For you also have realized that you likewise have many times cursed others.* Another reality that exists in life is that people will talk badly about us at times. Solomon encourages us not to pay attention to what others say. If we do hear them, we should not take them seriously. Of course, it is good to receive rebuke (7:5); but the wise man is not talking about constructive criticism but about one who is just speaking evil of another. He is telling us that we should not think of everything that others say as being so important that we listen in on conversations that are not intended for us. This can result in added stress for us. Furthermore, the wise man reminds us that we have done the same thing (cursed others). Again, he is not attempting to justify sin; but he offers this as a reminder that we ought to be careful about the conversations to which we try to listen.

7:23-24 *I tested all this with wisdom, and I said, "I will be wise," but it was far from me. What has been is remote and exceedingly mysterious. Who can discover it?* It is interesting to read of Solomon's determination to become wise. God had already granted him wisdom (1 Kings 3:12). There is an obvious difference, then, between worldly wisdom and heavenly wisdom. Solomon had, at least at one time, heavenly wisdom. Yet, as he departed from God, he sought after worldly wisdom. This is the wisdom he is talking about in these verses. Worldly wisdom seeks to know and understand that which is *"remote and exceedingly mysterious (deep, KJV)."* Yet his question – *"Who can discover it?"* – is meant to remind us that worldly wisdom *cannot* answer the deep questions of life which Solomon (as well as many others of every generation) was pondering. The wisdom of the world is insufficient. Only the wisdom that comes from above can provide us with satisfactory answers.

7:25 *I directed my mind to know, to investigate and to seek wisdom and an explanation, and to know the evil of folly and the foolishness of madness.* Solomon again states his goal. He sought wisdom. He endeavored to understand the meaning of life and why conditions exist as they did. Yet when he began this investigation, he did so without acknowledging the Lord. As has been hinted at already, and will be stated more clearly at the end, such an endeavor is futile without understanding our purpose before God.

7:26 *And I discovered more bitter than death the woman whose heart is snares and nets, whose hands are chains. One who is pleasing to God will escape from her, but the sinner will be captured by her.* Solomon certainly had plenty of experience with women, having *"seven hundred wives, princesses, and three hundred concubines"* (1 Kings 11:3). He was also well-acquainted with the trouble that can be caused by wicked women, as his wives were responsible for turning his heart away from the Lord (1 Kings 11:4). Solomon acknowledges elsewhere that a good and godly woman can be a great blessing (Proverbs 31:10-31). But a woman who would lead one into sin is *"more bitter than death."* One who seeks to please God must be careful not to allow evil women to have an influence over him. With God's instructions, one is generally in a good position to avoid such trouble. The sinner, one who has rejected God's instructions and has chosen to go his own way, is vulnerable.

7:27-28 *"Behold, I have discovered this,"* says the Preacher, *"adding one thing to another to find an explanation, which I am still seeking but have not found. I have found one man among a thousand, but I have not found a woman among all these.* Solomon is referring to his quest for wisdom as a whole. Like anyone might do, he took pieces of the puzzle and put them together to try to see the big picture. One who strives to see the big picture through worldly wisdom alone will keep seeking, but will not find it since the answers require that we look past life *under the sun*. The wise man again mentions women, at least the ones in his life, as providing no help in his search. Worldly women will not be able to provide such help. This was part of Solomon's problem.

7:29   *Behold, I have found only this, that God made men upright, but they have sought out many devices."* God is not to be blamed for the sins and shortcomings of man. In the beginning, God made Adam free of sin. Yet Adam eventually disobeyed the Lord. The same thing continues to happen. Adam's sin did not make every one of his descendants a sinner, as many have been led to believe. Instead, all of us have chosen wicked and worldly pursuits, thus departing from the upright and innocent state in which we were formed. As Paul would later write: *"Death spread to all men, because all sinned"* (Romans 5:12). We cannot blame God for sin or the consequences of sin.

Chapter 8

Civil Authorities (8:1-13)

8:1   *Who is like the wise man and who knows the interpretation of a matter? A man's wisdom illumines him and causes his stern face to beam.* After discussing the futility of wisdom and its limitations, the wise man reminds us that wisdom it still beneficial. As long as we understand the limitations, it is certainly appropriate to acquire and use wisdom. When Solomon asks – *"Who is like the wise man?"* – he is contrasting the wise man with the fallen man of the previous verse (7:29). Though many depart from uprightness and seek out many devices, the wise man will follow the Lord. Therefore, his wisdom results in enlightenment and boldness.

8:2   *I say, "Keep the command of the king because of the oath before God.* Solomon now begins a discussion about obedience to civil authorities. When studying this passage, it is important that we understand the context. When the Scriptures speak of our responsibility to obey authorities and the benefit we receive from authorities, it must be assumed that said authorities are satisfying their divinely-ordained role. Otherwise we may be forced to *disobey* the authorities (cf. Acts 5:29); and we may suffer harm as a consequence of their wickedness (Proverbs 29:2). This idea of our conditional obedience to civil authorities is suggested in this verse. We are to *"keep the command of the king"* for a specific reason. Just because he is king and claims authority over the nation? No, *"because of the oath before God."* We must consider God and His will first. Human law does not supersede divine law.

8:3   ***Do not be in a hurry to leave him. Do not join in an evil matter, for he will do whatever he pleases."*** The word *hurry* or *hasty* (KJV) is from a word that means to tremble or be alarmed. This makes sense in light of the next phrase: *"Do not join in an evil matter."* We have a divine obligation to obey the king to the extent which God allows us (see discussion on 8:2). Therefore, if we are doing right, both by the king and the Lord, we should not *"be in a hurry to leave him"* because we will not have a guilty conscience or have anything to hide. On the last phrase, *"he will do whatever he pleases,"* there is a question as to whether the one whom the king is seeking to please is the Lord or himself. In either case, the point for us is to serve the Lord and serve the king in order to avoid trouble.

8:4   ***Since the word of the king is authoritative, who will say to him, "What are you doing?"*** The king has authority over the people. Therefore, he is able to act and make laws without consulting the people. This does not mean that the king's words are infallible or that unjust decrees cannot be challenged or questioned. But it does mean that there will be consequences to challenging the king, particularly if he is *"an old and foolish king who no longer knows how to receive instruction"* (4:13).

8:5   *He who keeps a royal command experiences no trouble, for a wise heart knows the proper time and procedure.* One who obeys the law will have no trouble from those who make and enforce the laws. It is as Paul would later write: *"Do you want to have no fear of authority? Do what is good and you will have praise from the same"* (Romans 13:3). The one who is wise understands the times and procedures regarding how the rulers operate, which allows him to avoid unnecessary trouble.

8:6   *For there is a proper time and procedure for every delight, though a man's trouble is heavy upon him.* In the realm of activity that involves action from the civil authorities, the authorities have their proper time and procedure for carrying out their work. Those in need of assistance from the authorities, whose *"trouble is heavy upon* [them]," will have to wait for the *"proper time and procedure"* for help to come. As is often the case, the relief to be provided by those in authority is delivered much slower than it is needed or expected (see discussion on 5:8).

8:7   *If no one knows what will happen, who can tell him when it will happen?* Life is uncertain; therefore, plans and schedules often do not work out the way that man intends. This is important in this context, as it shows us that even those in positions of authority over us are not omniscient and cannot foresee and plan for every problem that will arise.

8:8   *No man has authority to restrain the wind with the wind, or authority over the day of death; and there is no discharge in the time of war, and evil will not deliver those who practice it.* The word that is translated *wind* may also be translated *spirit*, as it is in the King James Version. The context will determine which word is appropriate. As the wise man is discussing the uncertainty of life (8:7) and the *"day of death,"* it seems that *spirit* is the proper word to use here. The point is that when the *"day of death"* comes, one cannot restrain his spirit from returning *"to God who gave it"* (12:7). It is as a soldier who cannot be discharged from service when the nation is involved in a war. At death, one's spirit will depart from his body and return to the Lord. This reminder is good and necessary for all of us, particularly those who practice evil, as Solomon mentions at the end of the verse. Since deliverance does not come from wickedness, one should pause to consider his endeavors and his fate if he does not follow the Lord.

8:9   *All this I have seen and applied my mind to every deed that has been done under the sun wherein a man has exercised authority over another man to his hurt.* The one who is being hurt here is not the one being ruled, but the one who is ruling over others. Those who selfishly seek power do so in order to gain an advantage over others. Yet Solomon, in observing those things which were done *"under the sun,"* saw the negative consequences to possessing authority over others. However, when coupled with the next verse, we see a point about *wicked* rulers who, though they may have harmed others, will suffer harm themselves (see discussion on 4:1).

8:10   *So then, I have seen the wicked buried, those who used to go in and out from the holy place, and they are soon forgotten in the city where they did thus. This too is futility.* Though this principle may apply in some way to all wicked people, in the context it is referring to wicked rulers. Though they used to hold a position of power and could come and go as they pleased, their death would eventually come and they would not be able to prevent it (see 8:8). Though they wickedly exercised authority so that the people would fear them, once they were dead and buried, the people would forget them, thus nullifying what they attempted to accomplish in their lives.

8:11   *Because the sentence against an evil deed is not executed quickly, therefore the hearts of the sons of men among them are given fully to do evil.* Civil authorities have the divine obligation to punish evildoers. They are to be a *"cause of fear"* for those who do evil (Romans 13:3-4). But in order for this to be the case, the wise man says that the punishment for evil must be *"executed quickly."* When the execution of justice is not swift, it has a corrupting influence upon society. Punishment is not just for the evildoer. If it were, the timing of it would not matter so much. Punishment is also meant to deter those who might later do evil. When the punishment is swift, the memory of the crime is still fresh in the people's mind, impressing upon their minds the connection between the crime and the punishment. When punishment is delayed, the connection is not as apparent; or one may believe he can escape punishment, thus making the crime more attractive.

8:12-13 *Although a sinner does evil a hundred times and may lengthen his life, still I know that it will be well for those who fear God, who fear Him openly. But it will not be well for the evil man and he will not lengthen his days like a shadow, because he does not fear God.* Solomon mentioned the *"wicked man who prolongs his life in his wickedness"* in the previous chapter (7:15). This observation that the wicked are not getting what they deserve *in this life* can be discouraging to those who are trying to be righteous. Yet Solomon says that even if one prospers in this life despite his great wickedness, it is better to openly fear God. This is another passage in which he is implying that there is more to our existence than this life. In the grand scheme of things, regardless of what happens in the few days we have on the earth, it will be better for those who fear God than for those who practice wickedness.

Wisdom is Limited (8:14-17)

8:14   *There is futility which is done on the earth, that is, there are righteous men to whom it happens according to the deeds of the wicked. On the other hand, there are evil men to whom it happens according to the deeds of the righteous. I say that this too is futility.* After briefly mentioning the benefits of righteousness over wickedness that extend beyond this life, the wise man returns to the futility of life on the earth. In this verse he states his observation that the righteous suffer harm that we might think the wicked deserve. In the same way, the wicked often prosper over the righteous.

8:15   *So I commended pleasure, for there is nothing good for a man under the sun except to eat and to drink and to be merry, and this will stand by him in his toils throughout the days of his life which God has given him under the sun.* Knowing that life is short and unfair, Solomon recommends that one enjoy the pleasures of this life. This is not a contradiction of his earlier discussion of pleasure, in which he found it was futile and that it accomplished nothing (2:1-2). In the earlier discussion, he was seeking purpose in life. The pursuit of pleasure could not provide this. But when one uses pleasure as a way to distract himself from the troubles of life, while also remembering his true purpose and the eternal consequences of his behavior, it can be helpful. There is a time for such things (see 3:4), as long as we keep the right perspective about everything.

8:16-17 *When I gave my heart to know wisdom and to see the task which has been done on the earth (even though one should never sleep day or night), and I saw every work of God, I concluded that man cannot discover the work which has been done under the sun. Even though man should seek laboriously, he will not discover; and though the wise man should say, "I know," he cannot discover.* Solomon again discusses the limitations of man and his wisdom. Even though one may seek diligently, he cannot reach the level of God. Even if one is able to keep from sleeping and devotes his entire existence to such a pursuit, he will still be unable to know the mind of God apart from divine revelation.

Chapter 9

Man's Deeds Are in the Hands of God (9:1-9)

9:1 *For I have taken all this to my heart and explain it that righteous men, wise men, and their deeds are in the hand of God. Man does not know whether it will be love or hatred; anything awaits him.* After concluding the previous chapter with the reminder that God is greater than man, Solomon provides another reminder here of our accountability before God. The Lord sees our deeds and knows what lies before us. Man does not know whether *love or hatred* await him as he journeys on in life.

9:2 *It is the same for all. There is one fate for the righteous and for the wicked; for the good, for the clean and for the unclean; for the man who offers a sacrifice and for the one who does not sacrifice. As the good man is, so is the sinner; as the swearer is, so is the one who is afraid to swear.* It may seem a bit strange that Solomon is reverting back to a discussion that seems to focus exclusively on life *under the sun*. After spending the first six chapters focusing exclusively on the futility of life, he began making references to the eternal spirit of man and our need to look beyond this life (see 7:2-5; 8:12-13). Here he refers to the common fate of man in death. It is important to recognize the limited scope of his comments in these verses.

9:3   *This is an evil in all that is done under the sun, that there is one fate for all men. Furthermore, the hearts of the sons of men are full of evil and insanity is in their hearts throughout their lives. Afterwards they go to the dead.* The first phrase corresponds to the previous verse. The wise man says that this common fate is *evil*, meaning that it does not seem fair when the righteous are not rewarded and the wicked are not punished in this life. The next phrase – *"the hearts of the sons of men are full of evil"* – can be understood in light of what he has said earlier: *"Because the sentence against an evil deed is not executed quickly, therefore the hearts of the sons of men among them are given fully to do evil"* (8:11). Though the original context of that verse is about the failure of civil authorities to carry out their proper work, this is not an indictment of God for delaying His punishment of sinners. While it is true that many will respond to God's patience by proceeding *"from bad to worse"* (2 Timothy 3:13), some will take advantage of His patience and *"come to repentance"* (2 Peter 3:9). Solomon is not blaming God here for man's corrupt condition (see comments on 7:29), but is stating a fact: man, generally, is wicked; and ignoring the fate which comes after death, many do not see any real deterrent for sin. After a certain period of time, man goes to that common fate which we all share.

9:4   *For whoever is joined with all the living, there is hope; surely a live dog is better than a dead lion.* This is an important point to remember in this context. Solomon says the living have hope. Hope of what? He has just described our common fate in death, so the hope is not to somehow escape death. Rather, the hope is for something after death for those who serve the Lord. All the living have hope, even the wicked because they still have time to repent and practice what is right. If both the dog and the lion were living, the lion would be preferred. But at death, one's fate is sealed.

9:5   *For the living know they will die; but the dead do not know anything, nor have they any longer a reward, for their memory is forgotten.* This is a favorite verse of Jehovah's Witnesses and others who try to argue that at death the wicked cease to exist, rather than go on to punishment. What this verse is actually talking about is within the realm of the broader context – things which exist *under the sun*. Those who are alive are aware that their lives are temporary. Those who are dead have no more knowledge of what is done *under the sun*, can no longer enjoy the blessings of life, and will eventually be forgotten. The next verse makes it clear that Solomon is not teaching that the dead cease to exist, but that they simply perish from life on the earth.

9:6   *Indeed their love, their hate and their zeal have already perished, and they will no longer have a share in all that is done under the sun.* Again, the focus is on *"all that is done under the sun."* In regard to such things, the love, hate, and zeal of those who have passed on have perished. Those who are dead can no longer share in the blessings that exist *under the sun*.

9:7-8   *Go then, eat your bread in happiness and drink your wine with a cheerful heart; for God has already approved your works. Let your clothes be white all the time, and let not oil be lacking on your head.* Since we cannot enjoy the blessings that exist *under the sun* once we depart from this life, the wise man tells us to enjoy our blessings while we have them. The food, drink, clothing, and oil he mentions suggest a joyous and festive occasion. The phrase, *"for God has already approved your works,"* means that it is God's will that we enjoy those things with which He blesses us (see also 2:24; 3:13; 5:18-19).

9:9   *Enjoy life with the woman whom you love all the days of your fleeting life which He has given to you under the sun; for this is your reward in life and in your toil in which you have labored under the sun.* God designed marriage from the beginning to be a lifelong relationship between a man and a woman (Genesis 2:24; Matthew 19:4-6). Therefore, it is important that each spouse is faithful to his/her mate and live up to the marriage vows. But Solomon teaches here that even though it is to be a lifelong relationship, marriage is not something to be grudgingly endured after a couple grows apart from each other. Rather, we ought to *enjoy* our time with our mates as long as we live. This is God's design and is a great blessing to be enjoyed if we have the proper attitude toward our mates and the marriage relationship.

Work with All Your Might (9:10-12)

9:10   *Whatever your hand finds to do, do it with all your might; for there is no activity or planning or knowledge or wisdom in Sheol where you are going.* A few verses earlier, Solomon said of those who had died, *"their zeal [has] already perished, and they will no longer have a share in all that is done under the sun"* (9:6). But reminding us that our lives are temporary should not be dispiriting to us, causing us to abandon our labors in life because there is no lasting benefit from them. Rather, we are to work hard and take advantage of the time we have now. After we reach Sheol (the grave), there will be no more work, preparations, or learning to do. We will be judged based upon what we do in this life (see 12:14), not on what we do after this life. Therefore, we must do the best we can now to accomplish those things we ought to be doing.

9:11   *I again saw under the sun that the race is not to the swift and the battle is not to the warriors, and neither is bread to the wise nor wealth to the discerning nor favor to men of ability; for time and chance overtake them all.* This verse emphasizes the uncertainty of life. While we may work, prepare, learn, and gain experience – as mentioned in the previous verse – we cannot predict what will happen. At times, the faster runner is beaten, and the stronger warrior is defeated. Wisdom and talent do not guarantee favor or success. So while we ought to do the best we can (9:10), we must not become arrogant and ignore the uncertain nature of life. But it is important to notice why Solomon says unexpected things happen. It is not necessarily because God has some direct involvement in producing certain results (though that did happen at various times throughout the Bible). Rather, *time and chance* produce uncertain outcomes. Some want to attribute every event and circumstance in life to God, but the wise man clearly tells us that various outcomes in life are the result of coincidence and happenstance.

9:12   *Moreover, man does not know his time: like fish caught in a treacherous net and birds trapped in a snare, so the sons of men are ensnared at an evil time when it suddenly falls on them.* In the previous three verses, Solomon has reminded us that life is fleeting (9:9), that we are going to the grave (9:10), and that life is uncertain (9:11). As he concludes the thought here, he tells us that death can come at any time – suddenly and unexpectedly. Therefore, it is important to enjoy life, work hard, and – in the midst of the uncertainties of life – prepare for this event that is certain. While we do not know when death will come, we do know that it will come.

Wisdom Under the Sun (9:13-18)

9:13-15 *Also this I came to see as wisdom under the sun, and it impressed me. There was a small city with few men in it and a great king came to it, surrounded it and constructed large siegeworks against it. But there was found in it a poor wise man and he delivered the city by his wisdom. Yet no one remembered that poor man.* Solomon has noted earlier that wisdom is a greater source of strength than a city's rulers (7:19). Similarly, he says in this example that wisdom was able to deliver a city when a great king came to defeat it. But what is interesting is that Solomon says that this was not a large city with greater defenses, but rather a *"small city"* that would have been more easily defeated. Furthermore, it was a *"poor man"* who possessed the wisdom necessary to deliver the city. Sadly, though, the people did not remember the poor man who, by his wisdom, delivered them.

9:16   *So I said, "Wisdom is better than strength." But the wisdom of the poor man is despised and his words are not heeded.* Though the city was small, by wisdom it was able to overcome a king and army of great strength that would have defeated other larger cities. Yet man often ignores wise counsel when it comes from a source he does not expect – in this case, the poor man. Wisdom is not to be judged by who possesses it. It is valuable and useful, even if the one who possesses it is poor in terms of wealth.

9:17   *The words of the wise heard in quietness are better than the shouting of a ruler among fools.* Man often places too much trust in civil rulers. The fact that a ruler is publicly proclaiming a message or advocating a certain position does not mean that his words are rooted in wisdom. Oftentimes they are not. It is better to heed the words of the wise, even if they are spoken in private.

9:18   *Wisdom is better than weapons of war, but one sinner destroys much good.* The first phrase refers back to the point Solomon made earlier about wisdom delivering a small city from a great king (9:14-15). The second phrase is a sobering reminder of the damaging effects of sin. Despite all of the good that wisdom can provide, one sinner is able to undo much of it. So while *wisdom is better than weapons of war*, this also suggests to us that sin is more destructive than the same weapons of war.

Chapter 10

Foolishness (10:1-20)

10:1   *Dead flies make a perfumer's oil stink, so a little foolishness is weightier than wisdom and honor.* All of the time and effort put forth by the perfumer in making his oil and giving it a pleasant aroma are ruined by a few dead flies. In the same way, obtaining wisdom and honor requires a significant investment in time and effort. However, just a little foolishness is able to sour the reputation of an otherwise wise and honorable man and cause others to have an unfavorable impression of him.

10:2   *A wise man's heart directs him toward the right, but the foolish man's heart directs him toward the left.* This translation suggests that the hearts of the wise and foolish men direct them in opposite directions. This is certainly true. However, the King James Version suggests a different meaning. It reads, *"A wise man's heart is at his right hand; but a fool's heart at his left."* The *right hand* is used throughout Scripture in a positive way, describing a position of blessing (Genesis 48:13-20), power (Exodus 15:6), strength (Psalm 20:6), and honor (Psalm 110:1). Pursuing wisdom leads to such things. Following after foolishness leads us away from them.

10:3   *Even when the fool walks along the road, his sense is lacking and he demonstrates to everyone that he is a fool.* When the fool is among others, the wise man says *"his sense is lacking"* or *"his wisdom faileth him"* (KJV). Though he may think himself to be wise, the manner in which he conducts himself make it apparent to all observers that he is a fool.

10:4   *If the ruler's temper rises against you, do not abandon your position, because composure allays great offenses.* When Solomon instructs us not to abandon our position, place (KJV), or post in the face of a ruler's anger, it must be assumed that our current position is one that we ought to be holding. Therefore, when a ruler becomes angry against us, we should not immediately abandon our rightful position or post. The last phrase of this verse is quite different in the New American Standard ("composure allays great offenses") and the King James ("yielding pacifieth great offences") translations. Some commentators have interpreted this to mean that if we are calm and respectful before the authorities, then they will be more lenient or we will have an opportunity to make a defense when their tempers cools. However, this assumes we are pacifying the rulers, whereas the text says we pacify offenses. In his commentary on this verse, Delitzsch suggests that to pacify or allay offenses means not to commit them. This seems to fit with the context. By not abandoning his position and continuing to do what he ought to do, he keeps himself from committing other sins. The overall point of this verse is that we should not allow the anger of a ruler to rattle us and cause us to abandon what is right and forsake our obligations.

10:5-7 *There is an evil I have seen under the sun, like an error which goes forth from the ruler— folly is set in many exalted places while rich men sit in humble places. I have seen slaves riding on horses and princes walking like slaves on the land.* Because of the negative consequences associated with foolishness, especially compared with the benefits of wisdom, we might expect that those who act foolishly will either never attain to or will fall from positions of prominence. Yet folly (foolishness) is often found in exalted places, even though it is as out of place there as a slave who has exchanged places with a prince. Folly does not belong in that position. Solomon says that the exaltation of folly is an evil that exists under the sun. But he compares it to "an error which goes forth from the ruler." When a ruler issues a decree, no matter how foolish or sinful it is, it goes forth with the weight of the ruler's authority behind it. The wise man's point is that when we see folly in prominent positions, we should not think of this as a rare exception, for we will regularly and consistently see this happen.

10:8-9 *He who digs a pit may fall into it, and a serpent may bite him who breaks through a wall. He who quarries stones may be hurt by them, and he who splits logs may be endangered by them.* Life does not always turn out as we intend or desire. In any activity that man undertakes, there are risks involved. There are no guarantees of prosperity, success, or safety, despite one's best efforts. Even if one is not pursuing folly, evil or hardships may still befall him. The uncertainty that exists in life is a reality that must be recognized and considered.

10:10   *If the axe is dull and he does not sharpen its edge, then he must exert more strength. Wisdom has the advantage of giving success.* After mentioning the risks that are inevitable in physical labor, Solomon uses a related example to make a point about wisdom. Though a dull axe and a sharpened axe may both be able to accomplish their purpose in splitting a piece of wood, it is better to take the time to sharpen the axe. Using the dull axe requires more strength from the one using it and, with the extra effort necessary, poses a greater threat to one's safety. Wisdom, though it takes time to develop, is beneficial in the same way a sharpened axe is – it allows one to efficiently and effectively deal with the challenges of life.

10:11   *If the serpent bites before being charmed, there is no profit for the charmer.* This verse makes a point about the importance of timeliness in gaining and using wisdom. The previous verse makes the point about the benefit of wisdom with the analogy of the dull axe. This verse teaches that wisdom which might be gained in the future cannot help us in the present. Though a serpent might be charmed, until the charmer finishes that task, the threat remains of being bitten by the serpent. In the same way, though wisdom might be gained, until we obtain wisdom and apply it, we will be in danger of the hardships of life that come from lack of wisdom. The last phrase in the King James translation differs slightly: *"and a babbler is no better."* The point, however, is the same. The babbler is the fool who has not obtained wisdom. Though he and the wise man may both speak, the babbling of a fool will not dispel the threat of harm like the effective and timely words of the wise.

10:12-13 *Words from the mouth of a wise man are gracious, while the lips of a fool consume him; the beginning of his talking is folly and the end of it is wicked madness.* The words of the wise man will do him good. The words of the fool will destroy him. Solomon says that when the fool begins to speak, his words are useless and unhelpful. As he continues to speak – which he will inevitably do – he will only bring trouble upon himself.

10:14 *Yet the fool multiplies words. No man knows what will happen, and who can tell him what will come after him?* As noted in the previous verse, though the fool's words only serve to cause him trouble, he continues to speak. The second phrase in this verse is similar to the reminder given earlier about the limitations of those in positions of power (8:7). Since no one is able to accurately predict the future, we must exercise wisdom to be able to handle challenges that arise. However, the fool, in his arrogance, does not pause to consider, take counsel, or prepare. He simply keeps spouting his words of folly.

10:15 *The toil of a fool so wearies him that he does not even know how to go to a city.* In this analogy, Solomon describes the pursuit of foolishness as preventing one from entering a city – a place of safety and security in times of trouble. The fool, for all of his effort, remains vulnerable to the dangers that exist out in the world.

10:16 *Woe to you, O land, whose king is a lad and whose princes feast in the morning.* Trouble comes to a land when those in power do not rule with wisdom. The king is described as a *lad* because he lacks wisdom and does not have the experience necessary to effectively rule over the people. The time of the princes' feasting being in the morning is significant. When feasting begins in the morning, it suggests an abandonment of responsibility and the debauchery that will come from having more hours to devote to feasting (cf. Isaiah 5:11). The princes who feast in the morning are unconcerned with their obligations to the people and are only focused on enjoying *themselves* at the expense of the people of the land.

10:17   *Blessed are you, O land, whose king is of nobility and whose princes eat at the appropriate time—for strength and not for drunkenness.* The king of nobility is contrasted with the king who is a lad in the previous verse. The fact that he is *"the son of nobles"* (KJV) suggests that he has been trained properly how to handle such a position. Having been trained to rule wisely, he is a blessing to the land. The princes here, instead of feasting in the morning, *"eat at the appropriate time"* and for the appropriate purpose (*"for strength and not for drunkenness"*). Therefore, they do not require excessive taxing of the people for their own benefit, but only that which is reasonably necessary for them to do their work. The wise princes then focus on their work, which will help the people, rather than focusing solely on what they desire.

10:18   *Through indolence the rafters sag, and through slackness the house leaks.* The word translated *indolence* in the New American Standard is *slothfulness* in the King James Version. Anything that is gained or accomplished, if not maintained, will deteriorate and cause trouble. It is better to be diligent and maintain what has been accomplished, whether it is a house that has been built or wisdom that has been gained. This thought can be connected with the two previous verses. The land whose leaders are inexperienced and slothful will find itself in decline, especially compared with the land whose leaders are faithful, fair, and diligent in their work.

10:19   *Men prepare a meal for enjoyment, and wine makes life merry, and money is the answer to everything.* Any feasting that man may do – including the proper and improper feasting among the princes mentioned earlier (10:16-17) – is only able to provide a very limited benefit. Regardless of the reason one has for feasting – for strength (10:17), for excessive revelry (10:16), or simply for the purpose of enjoying the blessings which God has given (5:18-19) – the benefit derived from the feast lasts a very short time. In contrast, money – that which can be used to obtain goods and services one will need in the future – is able to provide a greater, long-term benefit. Solomon's point is not that money is somehow able to buy happiness. Rather, his point is about recognizing the proper value of the blessings and resources that we have.

10:20   *Furthermore, in your bedchamber do not curse a king, and in your sleeping rooms do not curse a rich man, for a bird of the heavens will carry the sound and the winged creature will make the matter known.* Solomon has already contrasted an inexperienced king with slothful princes (10:16) and a noble king with wise princes (10:17). In this verse, he does not make a distinction between the two. Regardless of the character of the king (or a rich man who would have a good deal of power and influence over others, including the king), we must be careful what we say, even while in secret. There are ways in which those words which are spoken in secret can find themselves out in the public and into the ears of those powerful persons about whom we have spoken. It is better to guard our speech at all times than to cause unnecessary trouble for ourselves.

Chapter 11

Looking Toward the Future (11:1-10)

11:1   *Cast your bread on the surface of the waters, for you will find it after many days.* The overall point of this verse is that there are certain things which we must do, even though we will not see the benefit from them until *"after many days."* The analogy most likely refers to the sowing of seed (that which will produce bread). In their comments on this verse, Jamieson, Fausset, and Brown explain it as seed which is cast "from boats into the overflowing waters of the Nile." As the water recedes, the seed takes root and begins to grow. This was commonly done in that area. Zerr suggests that this casting of seed on the waters is not common practice but something that must be done when conditions may seem unfavorable because one could not wait and see if the water would recede and then sow his seed. He would need to do what was necessary, even in less than ideal conditions. But whether this sowing refers to a common practice or one which is done under unfavorable circumstances, the point is the same: we must look past what is immediately before us and work to prepare for the future.

11:2   *Divide your portion to seven, or even to eight, for you do not know what misfortune may occur on the earth.*

To divide one's portion is to do good and be benevolent toward others. Seven is a complete number, yet Solomon says *"even to eight,"* emphasizing the importance of making every effort to help the less fortunate. The reason why we are to place such a great importance upon doing good for others is that we *"do not know what misfortune may occur."* Our ability to help others may not exist in the future like it does today. Furthermore, we may later find that we are in need of help ourselves. It is much easier for people to help those who have been known as being good, generous people.

11:3   *If the clouds are full, they pour out rain upon the earth; and whether a tree falls toward the south or toward the north, wherever the tree falls, there it lies.* There are many things in life that are simply out of our control. We cannot cause the rain, nor can we prevent the rain from coming. When the *"clouds are full"* or when conditions are such that the clouds will produce rain, it will rain, no matter what we do or what we think about it. When a tree falls, the direction in which it falls does not matter. If it falls one way, later conditions will not cause it to relocate to another place as if it had fallen there. So these things which are out of our control must simply be dealt with. It is pointless to worry about them and wish we could change the current conditions. We simply need to deal with the conditions as they exist.

11:4   *He who watches the wind will not sow and he who looks at the clouds will not reap.* After reminding us that life is uncertain (11:2) and that there are certain things which we cannot change (11:3), Solomon makes the point here that we cannot wait for some ideal circumstances to come along or eliminate every risk or hardship that may come. Seed needs to be sown so it can later be harvested. If this is not done, there will be no food with which one can feed himself and his family. Even if the wind is not blowing as we would wish and even though there may be a chance of rain, work must be done. We must be busy working while we can instead of wasting our time worrying about the future and being paralyzed by the uncertainty of life.

11:5   *Just as you do not know the path of the wind and how bones are formed in the womb of the pregnant woman, so you do not know the activity of God who makes all things.* Just as man cannot control many things in life, Solomon points out here that we cannot *know* everything about life. Certain things fall into the realm of the providential working of God. We cannot *"know the path of the wind"*; and even if we could, we would be powerless to change it. The way a child is formed and develops in the womb happens the way God designed for it to happen. So the wise man reminds us in the midst of the uncertainties of life, we should recognize God's place as Creator and Sustainer of all things.

11:6   *Sow your seed in the morning and do not be idle in the evening, for you do not know whether morning or evening sowing will succeed, or whether both of them alike will be good.* Because life is uncertain, we cannot base our future well-being upon overly optimistic predictions regarding our labors. It could be that under ideal conditions, one would be able to survive from the harvest of the seed that is sown in the morning alone. However, as Solomon has already pointed out, life is uncertain. It could be that the seed sown in the morning will not produce the fruit we hope that it will. Therefore, the wise man says we should sow in the morning and evening. This way, if one of these is unsuccessful, we have something to fall back on.

11:7-8 *The light is pleasant, and it is good for the eyes to see the sun. Indeed, if a man should live many years, let him rejoice in them all, and let him remember the days of darkness, for they will be many. Everything that is to come will be futility.* This statement is true when taken literally. Yet the light to which Solomon refers is not *daylight*, but it is life itself. His point: life and the blessings that come in it are good, and we ought to recognize and appreciate the blessings of life while we have them. As he reminds us again, the light of life is only temporary. The *"days of darkness"* are coming and *"will be many."* The phrase, *"days of darkness"* refers to the time after one's death (cf. Job 10:18-22). The wise man concludes his thought by reminding us that the things of this life are, ultimately, futile.

11:9 *Rejoice, young man, during your childhood, and let your heart be pleasant during the days of young manhood. And follow the impulses of your heart and the desires of your eyes. Yet know that God will bring you to judgment for all these things.* Because life is short and death is coming for all, the wise man encourages the *"young man"* to rejoice and enjoy life. He advises him to follow the impulses of his heart and the desire of his eyes. This is not to be seen as a permission to do anything that one might wish to do. There is still a standard – *"God will bring you to judgment."* Even in youth, we are obligated to act within the confines of God's laws. But as we serve God, we ought to enjoy our time and blessings here on the earth while we are able to do so.

11:10   *So, remove grief and anger from your heart and put away pain from your body, because childhood and the prime of life are fleeting.* There are many things in life which are out of our control. Solomon is not telling the young man that he can hope to remove everything that *causes* grief and anger in his life; he tells him to remove grief and anger themselves from his *heart*. He admonishes him to learn to control how he reacts to the difficult circumstances in life. Rather than responding with grief and anger, he should rejoice over the good things in life (11:9). And to whatever degree he is able, he should *"put away pain,"* or evil, from his life. He cannot completely remove every evil and vain thing from his life, but he must remove what he can so he can better focus on the things of God rather than the things of the world. Solomon expresses an urgency about this – *"childhood and the prime of life are fleeting."* As the wise man will go on to explain in the next chapter, one who refuses to accept and serve God during his youth will have difficulty turning to God later in life. Up until this point, Solomon has emphasized the day of death as the event for which we must prepare ourselves. But here he stresses the importance of starting to make these preparations early in life. While it is true that God will accept those of any age (young or old) who turn to Him, the earlier we can turn to God and serve Him, the better off we will be.

Chapter 12

Remember Your Creator in Your Youth (12:1-8)

12:1   *Remember also your Creator in the days of your youth, before the evil days come and the years draw near when you will say, "I have no delight in them";* The final two verses of the previous chapter are addressed to the *"young man."* This chapter begins with the same focus before shifting attention to the aged. While the young man is to enjoy life in his youth, he is also to remember that God will judge him for his youthful actions (11:9-10). Solomon admonishes the young man also to remember his Creator in his youth. Many young people want to focus on enjoying life and ignore God, thinking they will have time to seek spiritual things and make them a priority later in life. Yet even if one is fortunate enough to live to an old age, there is no guarantee that the spiritual things will seem all that important. One who ignores God and refuses to obey Him from his youth will have decades of bad habits, false beliefs, and misplaced priorities that have been ingrained into his being. While it is possible for an older man to turn to God after rejecting Him for years, it is very difficult to do. It is far better to turn to God and obey Him starting in one's youth.

12:2   *before the sun and the light, the moon and the stars are darkened, and clouds return after the rain;* The darkening of the sun, light, moon, and stars refers to one's death (see notes on 11:8). The following verses describe the various parts of one's physical body that begin to fail toward the end of life. Because of this, many try to extend the allegory into this verse and interpret the darkening of the sun, light, moon, and stars to one's vision becoming dim with age. Such an interpretation is certainly understandable, and there is no harm done to the passage by such a view. But the failing eyesight is mentioned in the following verse. It seems doubtful the wise man would mention it twice in this brief section. Therefore, the wise man is likely emphasizing the fact that death is much nearer late in life than it is in one's youth. The clouds returning after rain paint a dark, gloomy picture, signifying grief and mourning, which refer to the time after one's death when loved ones mourn his passing.

12:3   *in the day that the watchmen of the house tremble, and mighty men stoop, the grinding ones stand idle because they are few, and those who look through windows grow dim;* The watchmen (keepers of the house, KJV) who tremble are the hands that become shaky and unable to function as well as they once did. The mighty men who stoop are the legs that are no longer as stable as they once were. The grinding ones are the teeth that cannot be used as they once were, due in large part to the fact that they have become few. Those who look through the windows are the eyes which grow dim because the eyesight is failing.

12:4   *and the doors on the street are shut as the sound of the grinding mill is low, and one will arise at the sound of the bird, and all the daughters of song will sing softly.*

The doors that are closed to the street are likely referring to the lips that are used to keep the mouth closed while eating. With few teeth left to grind food, eating is difficult (hence the need for the mouth to be closed) and also quiet (likely because only soft food can be ingested). Arising at the sound of the bird refers to one's restless and broken sleep. The daughters of song are described as singing softly because the loss of hearing that one experiences with age makes their songs seem quieter.

12:5   *Furthermore, men are afraid of a high place and of terrors on the road; the almond tree blossoms, the grasshopper drags himself along, and the caperberry is ineffective. For man goes to his eternal home while mourners go about in the street.* Being afraid of high places refers to one becoming increasingly unsteady and, therefore, afraid of heights. Being afraid of terrors on the road alludes to the inability to defend against or escape from dangers away from home, either real or imagined. The almond tree blossoming describes the changing of one's hair color to gray and white. Zerr comments: "When an almond tree is in full bloom its top resembles the pale color of a head that is gray with age." The caperberry becoming ineffective refers to the loss of one's sexual desire. These berries were "used in ancient times; their repute as excitants of sexual desire is ancient and widespread" (International Standard Bible Encyclopedia). At the end of the decay that is described in these verses comes death. Solomon describes death as one going to his eternal home. The mourners will take to the street because one has passed on from this life. But he has not ceased to be; he simply has gone on to the place designated for him by God.

12:6-7 *Remember Him before the silver cord is broken and the golden bowl is crushed, the pitcher by the well is shattered and the wheel at the cistern is crushed; then the dust will return to the earth as it was, and the spirit will return to God who gave it.* After describing various ways in which one's physical body becomes worn out late in life, the wise man uses four analogies of death that signify its permanence and suddenness. While there is certainly a decline that one endures as he reaches the end of his life, the final moment itself will come suddenly. This should also serve as a reminder to the *young man* that Solomon began directing these thoughts toward (11:9-12:1). Death comes suddenly, no matter how much decay has happened up to that point. Whenever death comes, whether in one's youth or in one's old age, it is permanent. Therefore, all must *remember Him* (God) while we have life in which to do it. After death, the body (dust, see Genesis 2:7) will return to the earth while the spirit of man will return to God, the one who created our spirits and placed them within our temporary fleshly bodies.

12:8 *"Vanity of vanities," says the Preacher, "all is vanity!"* The wise man repeats the theme as he stated it at the beginning of the book (1:2). As the things of life decay and death eventually comes to all men, Solomon reminds us that the things that exist and are done *under the sun* are futile and of no lasting value. However, in light of this, he has said we must remember God (12:1, 6). Therefore, we must be looking past this life of vanity and looking to the things of God.

Purpose of This Book (12:9-12)

12:9-10 *In addition to being a wise man, the Preacher also taught the people knowledge; and he pondered, searched out and arranged many proverbs. The Preacher sought to find delightful words and to write words of truth correctly.* Though Solomon was wise, he did not seek to keep his wisdom to himself. As he had to learn some difficult lessons, he endeavored to impart the lessons he learned to others. This is why he refers to himself as *"the Preacher."* He was not keeping a personal diary that happened to be found by others after he was gone. The things that are written down in this book were meant for us. Solomon also describes the work that is involved in teaching others effectively. Though he possessed wisdom, it took effort on his part (pondering, searching out, arranging, seeking appropriate words, and writing the truth accurately) in order to impart his knowledge and wisdom to others.

12:11 *The words of wise men are like goads, and masters of these collections are like well-driven nails; they are given by one Shepherd.* The words of the wise that have been properly collected, arranged, and presented are like the goads used to direct cattle toward a certain place. The metaphor of the well-driven nails is used to describe the teachings becoming firmly fastened in one's mind. The Shepherd he refers to is God. His point is that the wisdom that he was teaching, which all men must accept and to which they must shape their lives, was from God. Solomon spent much time pursuing worldly wisdom (see 7:23-28), but it was not until he returned to the pursuit of the wisdom of God that he was able to discover his purpose in life.

12:12 *But beyond this, my son, be warned: the writing of many books is endless, and excessive devotion to books is wearying to the body.* The *"many books"* here is in contrast to the *"words of wise men"* which have been *"given by one Shepherd"* (12:11). Books are written after much study, learning, and reflection regarding the topics they address. Solomon's point is that as man continually devotes himself to worldly wisdom, he will never reach the point of perfect enlightenment. There will always be others who will come along and progress past those ideas that have previously been written down. Furthermore, the study of such writings is a tiring task. Pursuing worldly wisdom, whether as the writer or the reader, is a futile endeavor.

Man's Purpose in Life (12:13-14)

12:13 *The conclusion, when all has been heard, is: fear God and keep His commandments, because this applies to every person.* Based upon everything that Solomon had learned as he described in this book, this is the conclusion. Man's entire purpose is to fear and obey God. Ultimately, this is the only thing that matters in life. This applies to *every person*, meaning that there is no one who is exempt from this charge.

12:14 *For God will bring every act to judgment, everything which is hidden, whether it is good or evil.* Solomon gives the reason *why* all men must fear God and keep His commandments. God will judge the life of each person. There will be nothing *hidden* from Him, even though some things may have been kept secret from one's fellow man. Therefore, it matters little what others think of us, as they will never have a complete picture of all that we have done. God, however, knows all. He will judge us according to our deeds, whether they are good or evil. Though not explicitly stated, Solomon does imply that there will be a reward for goodness and a punishment for evil. If there were not, fearing and obeying God would be as vain as the rest of life *under the sun*. When one dies, his spirit returns to God (12:7). After death, as he points out in this verse, judgment will come (cf. Hebrews 9:27). Following judgment, man will go to his *"eternal home"* (12:5), which place will depend upon whether his deeds were good or evil. So all that matters in this life is fearing God and keeping His commandments (12:13). If we fail to do this, then our entire existence – not just life *under the sun*, but for eternity – will have been vain.

Closing Thoughts

Solomon described conditions in life that are true from generation to generation. The sun rises and sets (1:5); the wind blows and follows its circular course (1:6); the rivers flow into the sea (1:7); and *"there is nothing new under the sun"* (1:9). In the end, his conclusion was that man's purpose was to *"fear God and keep His commandments"* (12:13).

Is this still man's purpose today? Many religious people hold to the theory that man is saved by faith *alone*. If this were true, then it would be difficult to say that keeping God's commandments would be part of man's purpose today.

When Peter preached the gospel to Cornelius, he made a statement that parallels the conclusion of Solomon in Ecclesiastes. *"I most certainly understand now that God is not one to show partiality, but in every nation the man who fears Him and does what is right is welcome to Him"* (Acts 10:34-35). This passage makes it clear: those who will be accepted by God today are those who fear Him and keep His commandments (do what is right).

No one of accountable age will stand justified before God by faith *alone*. By faith, yes (Romans 5:1). But not by faith *alone*. James wrote, *"You see that a man is justified by works and not by faith alone"* (James 2:24). If we wish to be accepted by God, we must fulfill our purpose in fearing Him and obeying Him according to the gospel. The gospel is the message that the apostles were to take *"into all the world"* (Mark 16:15). In doing this, they were to *"make disciples of all the nations, baptizing them in the name of the Father and the Son and the Holy Spirit, teaching them to observe all that* [the Lord] *commanded"* (Matthew 28:19-20). Or, to put it another way, they were to teach all men to *"fear God and keep His commandments."* We must follow the same teaching today.

Works Referenced

Clarke, A. (2011). *Adam Clarke's Commentary* (Vol. 3) [Kindle version]. Available from Amazon.com

Cook, F. C., & Fuller, J. M. (1966). *The Bible Commentary (Barnes Notes on the Old Testament): Proverbs–Ezekiel*. Grand Rapids, MI: Baker Book House.

Delitzsch, F. (2001). *Commentary on the Old Testament* (Vol. 6). (M. G. Easton, Trans.). Peabody, MA: Hendrickson Publishers. (Original work published 1866-1891).

Etheridge, J. W. (1862). *The Targums of Onkelos and Jonathan Ben Uzziel on the Pentateuch*. Retrieved from http://archive.org/details/targumsonkelosa00ethegoog

Jamieson, R., Fausset, A. R., & Brown, D. (2011). *A Commentary, Critical and Explanatory, on the Old and New Testaments* [Kindle version]. Available from Amazon.com

Kidner, D. (1976). *The Message of Ecclesiastes*. Leicester, England: Inter-Varsity Press.

Masterman, E. W. G. (2010). Caperberry. In J. Orr (Ed.), *International Standard Bible Encyclopedia* [Kindle version]. Available from Amazon.com

Zerr, E. M. (1954). *Bible Commentary: Old Testament* (Vol. 2). Bowling Green, KY: Guardian of Truth Foundation.